D1368485

Cram101 Textbook Outlines to accompany:

Managing Quality: An Integrative Approach

Foster, 2nd Edition

An Academic Internet Publishers (AIPI) publication (c) 2007.

You have a discounted membership at www.Cram101.com with this book.

Get all of the practice tests for the chapters of this textbook, and access in-depth reference material for writing essays and papers. Here is an example from a Cram101 Biology text:

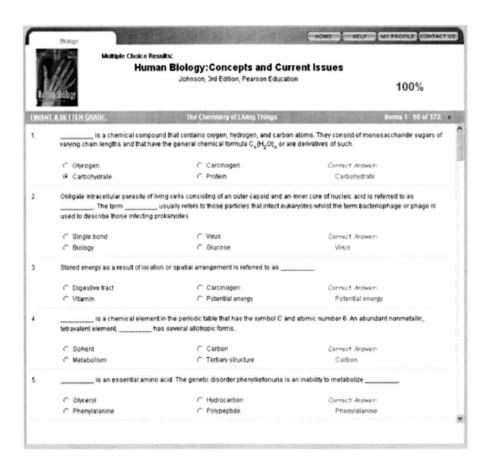

When you need problem solving help with math, stats, and other disciplines, www.Cram101.com will walk through the formulas and solutions step by step.

With Cram101.com online, you also have access to extensive reference material.

You will nail those essays and papers. Here is an example from a Cram101 Biology text:

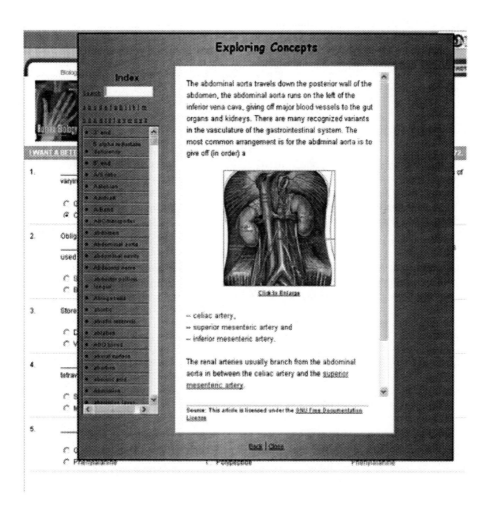

Visit **www.Cram101.com**, click Sign Up at the top of the screen, and enter DK73DW in the promo code box on the registration screen. Access to www.Cram101.com is normally $9.95, but because you have purchased this book, your access fee is only $4.95. Sign up and stop highlighting textbooks forever.

Learning System

Cram101 Textbook Outlines is a learning system. The notes in this book are the highlights of your textbook, you will never have to highlight a book again.

How to use this book. Take this book to class, it is your notebook for the lecture. The notes and highlights on the left hand side of the pages follow the outline and order of the textbook. All you have to do is follow along while your intructor presents the lecture. Circle the items emphasized in class and add other important information on the right side. With Cram101 Textbook Outlines you'll spend less time writing and more time listening. Learning becomes more efficient.

Cram101.com Online

Increase your studying efficiency by using Cram101.com's practice tests and online reference material. It is the perfect complement to Cram101 Textbook Outlines. Use self-teaching matching tests or simulate in-class testing with comprehensive multiple choice tests, or simply use Cram's true and false tests for quick review. Cram101.com even allows you to enter your in-class notes for an integrated studying format combining the textbook notes with your class notes.

Visit **www.Cram101.com**, click Sign Up at the top of the screen, and enter **DK73DW329** in the promo code box on the registration screen. Access to www.Cram101.com is normally $9.95, but because you have purchased this book, your access fee is only $4.95. Sign up and stop highlighting textbooks forever.

Managing Quality: An Integrative Approach
Foster, 2nd

CONTENTS

Preparation	Preparation refers to usually the first stage in the creative process. It includes education and formal training.
Effective communication	When the intended meaning equals the perceived meaning it is called effective communication.
Communication	Communication refers to the social process in which two or more parties exchange information and share meaning.
Product	Any physical good, service, or idea that satisfies a want or need is called product. Product in project management is a physical entity created as a result of project work.
Marketing	The American Marketing Association suggests that Marketing is "the process of planning and executing the pricing, promotion, and distribution of goods, ideas, and services to create exchanges that satisfy individual and organizational goals."
Accounting	The recording, classifying, summarizing, and interpreting of financial events and transactions to provide management and other interested parties the information they need to make good decisions is called accounting.
Financial management	The job of managing a firm's resources so it can meet its goals and objectives is called financial management.
Management	Management characterizes the process of leading and directing all or part of an organization, often a business, through the deployment and manipulation of resources. Early twentieth-century management writer Mary Parker Follett defined management as "the art of getting things done through people."
Manager	A person who is formally responsible for supporting the work efforts of other people is a manager.
Variance	In budgeting a variance is a difference between budgeted, planned or standard amount and the actual amount incurred/sold.
Contingency view	An extension of the humanistic perspective in which the successful resolution of organizational problems is thought to depend on managers' identification of key variables in the situation at hand is referred to as contingency view.
Quality management	Quality management is a method for ensuring that all the activities necessary to design, develop and implement a product or service are effective and efficient with respect to the system and its performance.
Quality dimension	A quality dimension refers to aspects of quality that help to better define what quality is. These include perceived quality, conformance, reliability, durability, and so on.
User-based	A definition of service or product quality that is customer centered is referred to as user-based.
Value-based	Value-based refers to a definition of quality relating to the social benefit from a product or service.
Efficiency	Efficiency refers to the use of minimal resources, such as raw materials, money, and people-to produce a desired volume of output.
Mutual fund	A mutual fund is a form of collective investment that pools money from many investors and invests the money in stocks, bonds, short-term money market instruments, and/or other securities. In a mutual fund, the fund manager trades the fund's underlying securities, realizing capital gains or loss, and collects the dividend or interest income.
Premium	Premium refers to the fee charged by an insurance company for an insurance policy. The rate of losses must be relatively predictable: In order to set the premium (prices) insurers must be able to estimate them accurately.
Conformance	A dimension of quality that refers to the extent to which a product lies within an allowable range of deviation from its specification is called the conformance.

Serviceability	A dimension of quality that refers to a product's ease of repair is referred to as serviceability.
Perceived quality	A dimension of quality identified by David Garvin that refers to a subjective assessment of a product's quality based on criteria defined by the observer is a perceived quality.
Brand image	The advertising metric that measures the type and favorability of consumer perceptions of the brand is referred to as the brand image.
Brand	A name, symbol, or design that identifies the goods or services of one seller or group of sellers and distinguishes them from the goods and services of competitors is a brand.
Advertising	Advertising refers to paid, nonpersonal communication through various media by organizations and individuals who are in some way identified in the advertising message.
Word of mouth	People influencing each other during their face-to-face converzations is called word of mouth.
Quality measures	Ratios that are used to measure a firm's performance in the area of quality management are referred to as quality measures.
Credibility	The extent to which a source is perceived as having knowledge, skill, or experience relevant to a communication topic and can be trusted to give an unbiased opinion or present objective information on the issue is called credibility.
Production	The creation of finished goods and services using the factors of production: land, labor, capital, entrepreneurship, and knowledge.
Personnel	A collective term for all of the employees of an organization. Personnel is also commonly used to refer to the personnel management function or the organizational unit responsible for administering personnel programs.
Client	The organizations with the products, services, or causes to be marketed and for which advertising agencies and other marketing promotional firms provide services is referred to as a client.
Trust	Trust refers to a legal relationship in which a person who has legal title to property has the duty to hold it for the use or benefit of another person. The term is also used in a general sense to mean confidence reposed in one person by another.
Empathy	Empathy refers to dimension of service quality-caring individualized attention provided to customers.
Industry	Industry refers to a group of firms offering products that are close substitutes for each other.
Service reliability	A dimension of service quality that refers to the ability of the service provider to perform the promized service dependably and accurately is service reliability.
Devise	In a will, a gift of real property is called a devise.
Strategic plan	The formal document that presents the ways and means by which a strategic goal will be achieved is a strategic plan. A long-term flexible plan that does not regulate activities but rather outlines the means to achieve certain results, and provides the means to alter the course of action should the desired ends change.
Alignment	Term that refers to optimal coordination among disparate departments and divisions within a firm is referred to as alignment.
Corporation	A form of business organization that is owned by owners, called shareholders, who have no inherent right to manage the business, and is managed by a board of directors that is elected by the shareholders is called a corporation.
Information system	An information system is a system whether automated or manual, that comprises people, machines, and/or methods organized to collect, process, transmit, and disseminate data that represent user information.
Users	Users refer to people in the organization who actually use the product or service purchased by the buying center.

Human resource management	The process of evaluating human resource needs, finding people to fill those needs, and getting the best work from each employee by providing the right incentives and job environment, all with the goal of meeting the needs of the firm are called human resource management.
Resource management	Resource management is the efficient and effective deployment of an organization's resources when they are needed. Such resources may include financial resources, inventory, human skills, production resources, or information technology.
Strategic planning	The process of determining the major goals of the organization and the policies and strategies for obtaining and using resources to achieve those goals is called strategic planning.
Productivity	Productivity refers to the total output of goods and services in a given period of time divided by work hours.
Cross-functional team	That which brings together persons from different functions to work on a common task is called a cross-functional team.
Strategic management	A philosophy of management that links strategic planning with dayto-day decision making. Strategic management seeks a fit between an organization's external and internal environments.
Human resources	Human resources refers to the individuals within the firm, and to the portion of the firm's organization that deals with hiring, firing, training, and other personnel issues.
Product design engineering	A form of engineering that involves activities associated with concept development, needs specification, final specification, and final design of a product is referred to as product design engineering.
Computer-aided design	Computer-aided design is the use of a wide range of computer-based tools that assist engineers, architects and other design professionals in their design activities. It is the main geometry authoring tool within the Product Lifecycle Management process and involves both software and sometimes special-purpose hardware.
Concurrent engineering	The simultaneous performance of product design and process design is concurrent engineering. Typically, concurrent engineering involves the formation of cross-functional teams. This allows engineers and managers of different disciplines to work together simultaneously in developing product and process designs.
Statistical thinking	Deming's concept relating to databased decision-making is statistical thinking. Statistical thinking is the tendency to want to understand complete situational understanding over a wide range of data where several control factors may be interacting at once to produce and outcome.
Contribution	In business organization law, the cash or property contributed to a business by its owners is referred to as contribution.
Statistical process control	Statistical process control is a method for achieving quality control in manufacturing processes. It is a set of methods using statistical tools such as mean, variance and others, to detect whether the process observed is under control.
Exhibit	Exhibit refers to a copy of a written instrument on which a pleading is founded, annexed to the pleading and by reference made a part of it. Any paper or thing offered in evidence and marked for identification.
Control process	A process involving gathering processed data, analyzing processed data, and using this information to make adjustments to the process is a control process.
Quality control	The measurement of products and services against set standards is referred to as quality control.
Operations management	A specialized area in management that converts or transforms resources into goods and services is operations management.
Organizational	The study of human behavior in organizational settings, the interface between human behavior and the

Behavior	organization, and the organization itself is called organizational behavior.
Systems view	A management viewpoint that focuses on the interactions between the various components that combine to produce a product or service is called systems view. The systems view focuses management on the system as the cause of quality problems.
Conversion	Conversion refers to any distinct act of dominion wrongfully exerted over another's personal property in denial of or inconsistent with his rights therein. That tort committed by a person who deals with chattels not belonging to him in a manner that is inconsistent with the ownership of the lawful owner.
Competitor	Other organizations in the same industry or type of business that provide a good or service to the same set of customers is referred to as a competitor.
Cost leadership	A type of competitive strategy with which the organization aggressively seeks efficient facilities, cuts costs, and employs tight cost controls to be more efficient than competitors is referred to as cost leadership.
Complaint	The pleading in a civil case in which the plaintiff states his claim and requests relief is called complaint. In the common law, it is a formal legal document that sets out the basic facts and legal reasons that the filing party (the plaintiffs) believes are sufficient to support a claim against another person, persons, entity or entities (the defendants) that entitles the plaintiff(s) to a remedy (either money damages or injunctive relief).
Tactic	A short-term immediate decision that, in its totality, leads to the achievement of strategic goals is called a tactic.
Knowledge technology	Knowledge technology refers to technology that adds a layer of intelligence to information technology, to filter appropriate information and deliver it when it is needed.
Organizational culture	Widely shared values within an organization that provide coherence and cooperation to achieve common goals are referred to as a organizational culture.
Comprehensive	A comprehensive refers to a layout accurate in size, color, scheme, and other necessary details to show how a final ad will look. For presentation only, never for reproduction.
Options	Options give the owner the right but not the obligation to buy or sell an underlying security at a set price for a given time period.
Sustainable competitive advantage	A strength, relative to competitors, in the markets served and the products offered is referred to as the sustainable competitive advantage.
Competitive advantage	A business is said to have a competitive advantage when its unique strengths, often based on cost, quality, time, and innovation, offer consumers a greater percieved value and there by diffetiating it from its competitors.
Yield	The interest rate that equates a future value or an annuity to a given present value is a yield.
Strategy formulation	The process of deciding on a strategic direction by defining a company's mission and goals, its external opportunities and threats, and its internal strengths and weaknesses is referred to as a strategy formulation.
Evaluation	The consumer's appraisal of the product or brand on important attributes is called evaluation.
Strategy implementation	Strategy implementation refers to the process of devising structures and allocating resources to enact the strategy a company has chosen.
Relationship management	A method for developing long-term associations with customers is referred to as relationship management.
Customer service	The ability of logistics management to satisfy users in terms of time, dependability, communication, and convenience is called the customer service.

Contingency theory	A theory that presupposes that there is no theory or method for operating a business that can be applied in all instances is referred to as contingency theory.
Competition	In business, competition occurs when rival organizations with similar products and services attempt to gain customers.
Nuclear Regulatory Commission	Federal agency that licenses the construction and opening of commercial nuclear power plants is called the Nuclear Regulatory Commission.
Voice of the customer	A term that refers to the wants, opinions, perceptions, and desires of the customer is a voice of the customer.
Complexity	The technical sophistication of the product and hence the amount of understanding required to use it is referred to as complexity. It is the opposite of simplicity.
Compromise	Compromise occurs when the interaction is moderately important to meeting goals and the goals are neither completely compatible nor completely incompatible.
Value chain	A tool, developed by Michael Porter that decomposes a firm into its core activities is called value chain. The value chain categorizes the generic value-adding activities of an organization. The "primary activities" include: inbound logistics, operations (production), outbound logistics, sales and marketing, and service (maintenance).
Asset	In business and accounting an asset is anything owned which can produce future economic benefit, whether in possession or by right to take possession, by a person or a group acting together, e.g. a company, the measurement of which can be expressed in monetary terms. Asset is listed on the balance sheet. It has a normal balance of debit.
Decline stage	The fourth and last stage of the product life cycle when sales and profits begin to drop is called the decline stage.
Product Life Cycle	A theoretical model of what happens to sales and profits for a product over time is the product life cycle.
Law of diminishing marginal returns	A law that stipulates that there is a point at which investment in quality improvement will become uneconomical is a law of diminishing marginal returns.
Economics	The study of how society chooses to employ resources to produce goods and services and distribute them for consumption among various competing groups and individuals is economics.
Enabling	Enabling refers to giving workers the education and tools they need to assume their new decision-making powers.
Participation	Participation refers to the process of giving employees a voice in making decisions about their own work.
Interest	Interest refers to the payment the issuer of the bond makes to the bondholders for use of the borrowed money. It is the return to capital achieved over time or as the result of an event.
Empowerment	Giving employees the authority and responsibility to respond quickly to customer requests is called empowerment.
Organizational design	The structuring of workers so that they can best accomplish the firm's goals is referred to as organizational design.
Organizational structure	Refers to how a company is put together and reflects some of the underlying ways that people interact with one another in and across jobs or departments is referred to as organizational structure.
Compensation	A payment that is given or recieved as reparation for a service or loss is referred to as compensation.

Go to **Cram101.com** for the Practice Tests for this Chapter.

Grievance	A charge by employees that management is not abiding by the terms of the negotiated labormanagement agreement is the grievance.
Arbitration	Arbitration is a form of mediation or conciliation, where the mediating party is given power by the disputant parties to settle the dispute by making a finding. In practice arbitration is generally used as a substitute for judicial systems, particularly when the judicial processes are viewed as too slow, expensive or biased. Arbitration is also used by communities which lack formal law, as a substitute for formal law.
Job analysis	Job analysis refers to a study of what is done by employees who hold various job titles. It refers to various methodologies for analyzing the requirements of a job.
Recruitment	Recruitment refers to the set of activities used to obtain a sufficient number of the right people at the right time; its purpose is to select those who best meet the needs of the organization.
Malcolm Baldrige National Quality Award	Malcolm Baldrige national quality award refers to U.S. national quality award sponsored by the U.S. Department of Commerce and private industry. The program aims to reward quality in the business sector, health care, and education, and was inspired by the ideas of Total Quality Management.
Vertical deployment	Vertical deployment refers to a term denoting that all of the levels of the management of a firm are involved in the firm's quality efforts.
Horizontal deployment	Horizontal deployment refers to a term that denotes that all of the departments of a firm are involved in the firm's quality efforts.
Performance appraisal	An evaluation in which the performance level of employees is measured against established standards to make decisions about promotions, compenzation, additional training, or firing is referred to as performance appraisal.
Total quality human resources management	Total quality human resources management refers to an approach to human resources management that involves many of the concepts of quality management. The primary purpose of this approach is to provide employees a supportive and empowered work environment.
Total Quality Management	The practice of striving for customer satisfaction by ensuring quality from all departments in an organization is called total quality management.
Materials management	Materials management refers to the activity that controls the transmission of physical materials through the value chain, from procurement through production and into distribution.
Three spheres of quality	Quality management, assurance, and control are referred to as three spheres of quality.
Quality assurance	Those activities associated with assuring the quality of a product or service is called quality assurance.
Value-added	A customer-based perspective on quality that is used by services, manufacturing, and public sector organizations is value-added. The concept of value-added involves a subjective assessment of the efficacy of every step in the process for the customer.
Assessment	Collecting information and providing feedback to employees about their behavior, communication style, or skills is an assessment.
Core	A core is the set of feasible allocations in an economy that cannot be improved upon by subset of the set of the economy's consumers (a coalition).
Electronic data interchange	Combine proprietary computer and telecommunication technologies to exchange electronic invoices, payments, and information among suppliers, manufacturers, and retailers is referred to as the electronic data interchange.
Contingency	Contingency approach refers to the dominant perspective in organizational behavior, it argues that

approach	there's no single best way to manage behavior. What 'works' in any given context depends on the complex interplay between a variety of person and situational factors.
Contingency perspective	Contingency perspective suggests that, in most organizations, situations and outcomes are contingent on, or influenced by, other variables.

Quality management	Quality management is a method for ensuring that all the activities necessary to design, develop and implement a product or service are effective and efficient with respect to the system and its performance.
Management	Management characterizes the process of leading and directing all or part of an organization, often a business, through the deployment and manipulation of resources. Early twentieth-century management writer Mary Parker Follett defined management as "the art of getting things done through people."
Empowerment	Giving employees the authority and responsibility to respond quickly to customer requests is called empowerment.
Franchise	A business established or operated under an authorization to sell or distribute a company's goods or services in a particular area is a franchise.
Manager	A person who is formally responsible for supporting the work efforts of other people is a manager.
Authority	Authority in agency law, refers to an agent's ability to affect his principal's legal relations with third parties. Also used to refer to an actor's legal power or ability to do something. In addition, sometimes used to refer to a statute, case, or other legal source that justifies a particular result.
Credibility	The extent to which a source is perceived as having knowledge, skill, or experience relevant to a communication topic and can be trusted to give an unbiased opinion or present objective information on the issue is called credibility.
Industry	Industry refers to a group of firms offering products that are close substitutes for each other.
Quality control	The measurement of products and services against set standards is referred to as quality control.
Product	Any physical good, service, or idea that satisfies a want or need is called product. Product in project management is a physical entity created as a result of project work.
Customer service	The ability of logistics management to satisfy users in terms of time, dependability, communication, and convenience is called the customer service.
Quality assurance	Those activities associated with assuring the quality of a product or service is called quality assurance.
Misuse	A defense that relieves a seller of product liability if the user abnormally misused the product is called misuse. Products must be designed to protect against foreseeable misuse.
Quality at the source	A method of process control whereby each worker is responsible for his or her own work and performs needed inspections at each stage of the process is referred to as the quality at the source.
Total cost	The total expense incurred by a firm in producing and marketing a product is the total cost. Total cost is the sum of fixed cost and variable cost. In physical distribution decisions, the sum of all applicable costs for logistical activities.
Loyalty	Marketers tend to define customer loyalty as making repeat purchases. Some argue that it should be defined attitudinally as a strongly positive feeling about the brand.
Trust	Trust refers to a legal relationship in which a person who has legal title to property has the duty to hold it for the use or benefit of another person. The term is also used in a general sense to mean confidence reposed in one person by another.
Competition	In business, competition occurs when rival organizations with similar products and services

attempt to gain customers.

Stock	In financial terminology, stock is the capital raized by a corporation, through the issuance and sale of shares. A shareholder is any person or organization which owns one or more shares of a corporation's stock. The aggregate value of a corporation's issued shares is its market capitalization.
Just-in-time	Just In Time (JIT) is an inventory strategy implemented to improve the return on investment of a business by reducing in-process inventory and its associated costs.
Purchasing	Purchasing refers to the function in a firm that searches for quality material resources, finds the best suppliers, and negotiates the best price for goods and services.
Malcolm Baldrige National Quality Award	Malcolm Baldrige national quality award refers to U.S. national quality award sponsored by the U.S. Department of Commerce and private industry. The program aims to reward quality in the business sector, health care, and education, and was inspired by the ideas of Total Quality Management.
Production	The creation of finished goods and services using the factors of production: land, labor, capital, entrepreneurship, and knowledge.
Productivity	Productivity refers to the total output of goods and services in a given period of time divided by work hours.
Budget	A financial plan that sets forth management's expectations for revenues and, based on those expectations, allocates the use of specific resources throughout the firm is called budget.
Status quo	The existing state of things is the status quo. In contract law, returning a party to status quo or status quo ante means putting him in the position he was in before entering the contract.
Reengineering	The fundamental rethinking and radical redesign of organizational processes to achieve dramatic improvements in critical measures of performance is reengineering.
Downsizing	The process of eliminating managerial and non-managerial positions are called downsizing.
Policy	Similar to a script in that a policy can be a less than completely rational decision-making method. Involves the use of a pre-existing set of decision steps for any problem that presents itself.
Staffing	Staffing refers to a management function that includes hiring, motivating, and retaining the best people available to accomplish the company's objectives.
Marketing	The American Marketing Association suggests that Marketing is "the process of planning and executing the pricing, promotion, and distribution of goods, ideas, and services to create exchanges that satisfy individual and organizational goals."
Departmental approach to design	An approach to design that requires product designers, marketers, process designers, and production managers to work through organizational lines of authority to perform work is a departmental approach to design.
Alignment	Term that refers to optimal coordination among disparate departments and divisions within a firm is referred to as alignment.
Strategic goal	A strategic goal is a broad statement of where an organization wants to be in the future; pertains to the organization as a whole rather than to specific divisions or departments.
Performance appraisal	An evaluation in which the performance level of employees is measured against established standards to make decisions about promotions, compenzation, additional training, or firing is referred to as performance appraisal.
Self-directed	Self-directed work team refers to a team made up of a group of employees who share

18

work team	responsibility for a complete product or process, or accomplishment of a significant part of a process. The self-directed work team literally directs its own work and manages its own work performance.
Exhibit	Exhibit refers to a copy of a written instrument on which a pleading is founded, annexed to the pleading and by reference made a part of it. Any paper or thing offered in evidence and marked for identification.
Organizational learning	Organizational learning is an area of knowledge within organizational theory that studies models and theories about the way an organization learns and adapts.
Strategic planning	The process of determining the major goals of the organization and the policies and strategies for obtaining and using resources to achieve those goals is called strategic planning.
Continuous improvement	Constantly improving the way the organization does things so that customer needs can be better satisfied is referred to as continuous improvement.
Hierarchy	A system of grouping people in an organization according to rank from the top down in which all subordinate managers must report to one person is called a hierarchy.
Jargon	Jargon is terminology, much like slang, that relates to a specific activity, profession, or group. It develops as a kind of shorthand, to express ideas that are frequently discussed between members of a group, and can also have the effect of distinguishing those belonging to a group from those who are not.
Adoption	In corporation law, a corporation's acceptance of a pre-incorporation contract by action of its board of directors, by which the corporation becomes liable on the contract, is referred to as adoption.
Pareto analysis	Pareto analysis is a statistical technique in decision making used for selection of a limited number of tasks that produce significant overall effect.
Basic seven tools of quality	Basic seven tools of quality refers to the fundamental methods for gathering and analyzing quality related data. They are: fishbone diagrams, histograms, Pareto analysis, flowcharts, scatter plots, run charts, and control charts.
Contribution	In business organization law, the cash or property contributed to a business by its owners is referred to as contribution.
Grant	Grant refers to an intergovernmental transfer of funds . Since the New Deal, state and local governments have become increasingly dependent upon federal grants for an almost infinite variety of programs.
Context	The effect of the background under which a message often takes on more and richer meaning is a context. Context is especially important in cross-cultural interactions because some cultures are said to be high context or low context.
Organizational commitment	A person's identification with and attachment to an organization is called organizational commitment.
Protectionism	The practice of shielding one or more sectors of a country's economy from foreign competition through the use of tariffs or quotas is protectionism.
Corporation	A form of business organization that is owned by owners, called shareholders, who have no inherent right to manage the business, and is managed by a board of directors that is elected by the shareholders is called a corporation.
Quality measures	Ratios that are used to measure a firm's performance in the area of quality management are referred to as quality measures.

Go to **Cram101.com** for the Practice Tests for this Chapter.

Committee	A long-lasting, sometimes permanent team in the organization structure created to deal with tasks that recur regularly is the committee.
Human resources	Human resources refers to the individuals within the firm, and to the portion of the firm's organization that deals with hiring, firing, training, and other personnel issues.
Taguchi	Taguchi is an engineer and statistician who developed a methodology for applying statistics to improve the quality of manufactured goods. Taguchi methods have been controversial among many conventional Western statisticians.
Acceptance	The actual or implied receipt and retention of that which is tendered or offered is the acceptance.
Quality loss function	A function that determines economic penalties that the customer incurs as a result of purchasing a nonconforming product is referred to as quality loss function.
Conformance	A dimension of quality that refers to the extent to which a product lies within an allowable range of deviation from its specification is called the conformance.
Ideal quality	A reference point identified by Taguchi for determining the quality level of a product or service is ideal quality.
Tangible	Having a physical existence is referred to as the tangible. Personal property other than real estate, such as cars, boats, stocks, or other assets.
Loss to society	Loss to society refers to, according to Taguchi, every time a dimension in a product varies from its target dimension.
Concept design	The process of determining which technologies and processes will be used to produce a product is called concept design.
Parameter design	Designing control factors such as product specifications and measurements for optimal product function is called parameter design.
Principal	In agency law, one under whose direction an agent acts and for whose benefit that agent acts is a principal.
Benchmarking	Discovering how others do something better than your own firm so you can imitate or leapfrog competition is called benchmarking.
Best practice	In business management, a best practice is a generally accepted "best way of doing a thing". A best practice is formulated after the study of specific business or organizational case studies to determine the most broadly effective and efficient means of organizing a system or performing a function.
Case study	A case study is a particular method of qualitative research. Rather than using large samples and following a rigid protocol to examine a limited number of variables, case study methods involve an in-depth, longitudinal examination of a single instance or event: a case. They provide a systematic way of looking at events, collecting data, analyzing information, and reporting the results.
Entrepreneurship	Entrepreneurship is the practice of starting new organizations, particularly new businesses generally in response to identified opportunities. Entrepreneurship is often a difficult undertaking, as a majority of new businesses fail.
Competencies	An organization's special capabilities, including skills, technologies, and resources that distinguish it from other organizations are competencies.
Core	A core is the set of feasible allocations in an economy that cannot be improved upon by subset of the set of the economy's consumers (a coalition).
Collaboration	Collaboration occurs when the interaction between groups is very important to goal attainment

and the goals are compatible. Wherein people work together —applying both to the work of individuals as well as larger collectives and societies.

Business case	The business case addresses, at a high level, the business need that a project seeks to resolve. It includes the reasons for the project, the expected business benefits, the options considered (with reasons for rejecting or carrying forward each option), the expected costs of the project, a gap analysis and the expected risks.
Empathy	Empathy refers to dimension of service quality-caring individualized attention provided to customers.
Competitor	Other organizations in the same industry or type of business that provide a good or service to the same set of customers is referred to as a competitor.
Organizational structure	Refers to how a company is put together and reflects some of the underlying ways that people interact with one another in and across jobs or departments is referred to as organizational structure.
Contingency perspective	Contingency perspective suggests that, in most organizations, situations and outcomes are contingent on, or influenced by, other variables.
Contingency approach	Contingency approach refers to the dominant perspective in organizational behavior, it argues that there's no single best way to manage behavior. What 'works' in any given context depends on the complex interplay between a variety of person and situational factors.
Indirect cost	A cost that is incurred for common or joint objectives and therefore can not be identified readily and specifically with a particular project is an indirect cost.
Design phase	The phase in the instructional system design process where learning objectives, tests, and the required skills and knowledge for a task are constructed and sequenced is the design phase.
Competitive advantage	A business is said to have a competitive advantage when its unique strengths, often based on cost, quality, time, and innovation, offer consumers a greater percieved value and there by diffetiating it from its competitors.
Key business factors	Those measures or indicators that are significantly related to the business success of a particular firm are called key business factors.
Teamwork	That which occurs when group members work together in ways that utilize their skills well to accomplish a purpose is called teamwork.
Forming	The first stage of team development, where the team is formed and the objectives for the team are set is referred to as forming.
Corporate philosophy	The values and 'rules of conduct' for running an organization are a corporate philosophy.
Team building	A term that describes the process of identifying roles for team members and helping the team members succeed in their roles is called team building.

International trade	The export of goods and services from a country and the import of goods and services into a country is referred to as the international trade.
Perceived quality	A dimension of quality identified by David Garvin that refers to a subjective assessment of a product's quality based on criteria defined by the observer is a perceived quality.
Globalization	Trend away from distinct national economic units and toward one huge global market is called globalization. Globalization is caused by four fundamental forms of capital movement throughout the global economy.
Trade deficit	Trade deficit refers to an unfavorable balance of trade; occurs when the value of a country's imports exceeds that of its exports.
Licensing	Licensing is a form of strategic alliance which involves the sale of a right to use certain proprietary knowledge (so called intellectual property) in a defined way.
Corporation	A form of business organization that is owned by owners, called shareholders, who have no inherent right to manage the business, and is managed by a board of directors that is elected by the shareholders is called a corporation.
Product	Any physical good, service, or idea that satisfies a want or need is called product. Product in project management is a physical entity created as a result of project work.
Trademark	A distinctive word, name, symbol, device, or combination thereof, which enables consumers to identify favored products or services and which may find protection under state or federal law is a trademark.
Marketing	The American Marketing Association suggests that Marketing is "the process of planning and executing the pricing, promotion, and distribution of goods, ideas, and services to create exchanges that satisfy individual and organizational goals."
Partnership	In the common law, a partnership is a type of business structure in which partners share with each other the profits or losses of the business undertaking in which they have all invested.
Capital	Contributions of money and other property to a business made by the owners of the business are capital.
Trust	Trust refers to a legal relationship in which a person who has legal title to property has the duty to hold it for the use or benefit of another person. The term is also used in a general sense to mean confidence reposed in one person by another.
Exporting	Selling products to another country is called exporting.
Production	The creation of finished goods and services using the factors of production: land, labor, capital, entrepreneurship, and knowledge.
Task environment	Task environment includes specific organizations, groups, and individuals that influence the organization.
Compensation	A payment that is given or recieved as reparation for a service or loss is referred to as compensation.
International law	Law that governs affairs between nations and that regulates transactions between individuals and businesses of different countries is an international law.
Customs	Customs is an authority or agency in a country responsible for collecting customs duties and for controlling the flow of people, animals and goods (including personal effects and hazardous items) in and out of the country.
Communication	Communication refers to the social process in which two or more parties exchange information and share meaning.

Go to **Cram101.com** for the Practice Tests for this Chapter.

Quality management	Quality management is a method for ensuring that all the activities necessary to design, develop and implement a product or service are effective and efficient with respect to the system and its performance.
Management	Management characterizes the process of leading and directing all or part of an organization, often a business, through the deployment and manipulation of resources. Early twentieth-century management writer Mary Parker Follett defined management as "the art of getting things done through people."
Complexity	The technical sophistication of the product and hence the amount of understanding required to use it is referred to as complexity. It is the opposite of simplicity.
Decentralization	Decentralization is the process of redistributing decision-making closer to the point of service or action.
Patent	A patent is a set of exclusive rights granted by a state to a person for a fixed period of time in exchange for the regulated, public disclosure of certain details of a device, method, process or composition of matter which is new, inventive, and useful or industrially applicable.
Productivity	Productivity refers to the total output of goods and services in a given period of time divided by work hours.
Exporter	A firm that sells its product in another country is an exporter.
Tariff	A tax or duty imposed on goods by a nation when the goods are imported into that nation is referred to as tariff.
Distribution	Distribution is one of the four aspects of marketing. A distribution business is the middleman between the manufacturer and retailer or (usually)in commercial or industrial the business customer.
Interest	Interest refers to the payment the issuer of the bond makes to the bondholders for use of the borrowed money. It is the return to capital achieved over time or as the result of an event.
Malcolm Baldrige National Quality Award	Malcolm Baldrige national quality award refers to U.S. national quality award sponsored by the U.S. Department of Commerce and private industry. The program aims to reward quality in the business sector, health care, and education, and was inspired by the ideas of Total Quality Management.
Options	Options give the owner the right but not the obligation to buy or sell an underlying security at a set price for a given time period.
Assessment	Collecting information and providing feedback to employees about their behavior, communication style, or skills is an assessment.
Customer retention	Customer retention refers to the percentage of customers who return to a service provider or continue to purchase a manufactured product.
Benchmarking	Discovering how others do something better than your own firm so you can imitate or leapfrog competition is called benchmarking.
Baldrige-qualified	Term used by firms that have been granted a site visit by the judges in the Malcolm Baldrige National Quality Award competition is baldrige-qualified.
Alignment	Term that refers to optimal coordination among disparate departments and divisions within a firm is referred to as alignment.
Organizational strategy	The process of positioning the Organization in the competitive environment and implementing actions to compete successfully is an organizational strategy.
Innovation	The process of creating and doing new things that are introduced into the marketplace as

products, processes, or services is innovation.

Strategic goal	A strategic goal is a broad statement of where an organization wants to be in the future; pertains to the organization as a whole rather than to specific divisions or departments.
Strategic planning	The process of determining the major goals of the organization and the policies and strategies for obtaining and using resources to achieve those goals is called strategic planning.
Management by fact	A core value of the Baldrige award that focuses on data-based decision making is management by fact.
Applicant	In many tribunal and administrative law suits, the person who initiates the claim is called the applicant.
Corporate citizenship	A theory of responsibility that says a business has a responsibility to do good is corporate citizenship. Terms used in the business sector to refer to business giving, ie. business relationships and partnerships with not-for-profit organizations.
Strategic plan	The formal document that presents the ways and means by which a strategic goal will be achieved is a strategic plan. A long-term flexible plan that does not regulate activities but rather outlines the means to achieve certain results, and provides the means to alter the course of action should the desired ends change.
Competition	In business, competition occurs when rival organizations with similar products and services attempt to gain customers.
Human resources	Human resources refers to the individuals within the firm, and to the portion of the firm's organization that deals with hiring, firing, training, and other personnel issues.
Stock	In financial terminology, stock is the capital raized by a corporation, through the issuance and sale of shares. A shareholder is any person or organization which owns one or more shares of a corporation's stock. The aggregate value of a corporation's issued shares is its market capitalization.
Loyalty	Marketers tend to define customer loyalty as making repeat purchases. Some argue that it should be defined attitudinally as a strongly positive feeling about the brand.
Customer contact	Customer contact refers to a characteristic of services that notes that customers tend to be more involved in the production of services than they are in manufactured goods.
Complaint	The pleading in a civil case in which the plaintiff states his claim and requests relief is called complaint. In the common law, it is a formal legal document that sets out the basic facts and legal reasons that the filing party (the plaintiffs) believes are sufficient to support a claim against another person, persons, entity or entities (the defendants) that entitles the plaintiff(s) to a remedy (either money damages or injunctive relief).
Customer service	The ability of logistics management to satisfy users in terms of time, dependability, communication, and convenience is called the customer service.
Asset	In business and accounting an asset is anything owned which can produce future economic benefit, whether in possession or by right to take possession, by a person or a group acting together, e.g. a company, the measurement of which can be expressed in monetary terms. Asset is listed on the balance sheet. It has a normal balance of debit.
Stretch target	A challenging goal or objective requiring significant effort to achieve is a stretch target.
Participation	Participation refers to the process of giving employees a voice in making decisions about their own work.
Performance	The process of providing employees with information regarding their performance effectiveness

feedback	is referred to as performance feedback.
Personnel	A collective term for all of the employees of an organization. Personnel is also commonly used to refer to the personnel management function or the organizational unit responsible for administering personnel programs.
Acceptance	The actual or implied receipt and retention of that which is tendered or offered is the acceptance.
Exhibit	Exhibit refers to a copy of a written instrument on which a pleading is founded, annexed to the pleading and by reference made a part of it. Any paper or thing offered in evidence and marked for identification.
Competitor	Other organizations in the same industry or type of business that provide a good or service to the same set of customers is referred to as a competitor.
Full-baldrige approach	Term used to depict states' quality award programs using the same criteria as the Malcolm Baldrige National Quality Award is referred to as full-baldrige approach.
Baldrige-lite	Term used to depict states' quality award programs using the same criteria as the Malcolm is referred to as the baldrige-lite.
Deming prize	Japanese quality award for individuals and groups that have contributed to the field of quality control is called the deming prize.
Statistical process control	Statistical process control is a method for achieving quality control in manufacturing processes. It is a set of methods using statistical tools such as mean, variance and others, to detect whether the process observed is under control.
Quality control	The measurement of products and services against set standards is referred to as quality control.
Committee	A long-lasting, sometimes permanent team in the organization structure created to deal with tasks that recur regularly is the committee.
Small business	Small business refers to a business that is independently owned and operated, is not dominant in its field of operation, and meets certain standards of size in terms of employees or annual receipts.
Policy	Similar to a script in that a policy can be a less than completely rational decision-making method. Involves the use of a pre-existing set of decision steps for any problem that presents itself.
Authority	Authority in agency law, refers to an agent's ability to affect his principal's legal relations with third parties. Also used to refer to an actor's legal power or ability to do something. In addition, sometimes used to refer to a statute, case, or other legal source that justifies a particular result.
Statistical thinking	Deming's concept relating to databased decision-making is statistical thinking. Statistical thinking is the tendency to want to understand complete situational understanding over a wide range of data where several control factors may be interacting at once to produce and outcome.
Quality assurance	Those activities associated with assuring the quality of a product or service is called quality assurance.
Tangible	Having a physical existence is referred to as the tangible. Personal property other than real estate, such as cars, boats, stocks, or other assets.
Contribution	In business organization law, the cash or property contributed to a business by its owners is referred to as contribution.

Just-in-time	Just In Time (JIT) is an inventory strategy implemented to improve the return on investment of a business by reducing in-process inventory and its associated costs.
Systems view	A management viewpoint that focuses on the interactions between the various components that combine to produce a product or service is called systems view. The systems view focuses management on the system as the cause of quality problems.
Visibility	Visibility is used in marketing, as a measure of how much the public sees a product or its advertising.
Inventory	Inventory refers to physical material purchased from suppliers, which may or may not be reworked for sale to customers. A unique element of services-the need for and cost of having a service provider available.
Work-in-process inventory	Inventory composed of the materials that still are moving through the stages of the production process is called work-in-process inventory.
Andon	Andon refers to the warning lights on an assembly line that light up when a defect occurs. When the lights go on, the assembly line is usually stopped until the problem is diagnosed and corrected.
Line-stop authority	The approval authority to stop a production line whenever a problem is detected is called line-stop authority.
In-process inspection	The practice of inspecting work, by the workers themselves, at each stage of the production process is an in-process inspection.
Acceptance sampling	Acceptance sampling refers to an inspection of a sample from a lot to decide whether to accept or not accept that lot.
Sampling plan	In market research, the determination of how the data is to be collected, the interval of data collection, and the subjects from whom the data will be collected is called a sampling plan.
Organizational commitment	A person's identification with and attachment to an organization is called organizational commitment.
Vertical deployment	Vertical deployment refers to a term denoting that all of the levels of the management of a firm are involved in the firm's quality efforts.
Horizontal deployment	Horizontal deployment refers to a term that denotes that all of the departments of a firm are involved in the firm's quality efforts.
Quality circle	A quality circle is a volunteer group composed of workers who meet together to discuss workplace improvement, and make presentations to management with their ideas.
Preventive maintenance	Maintaining scheduled upkeep and improvement to equipment so equipment can actually improve with age is called the preventive maintenance.
Career planning	Process in which individuals evaluate their abilities and interests, consider alternative career opportunities, establish career goals, and plan practical development activities is referred to as career planning.
Social responsibility	Social responsibility is a doctrine that claims that an entity whether it is state, government, corporation, organization or individual has a responsibility to society.
Conformance	A dimension of quality that refers to the extent to which a product lies within an allowable range of deviation from its specification is called the conformance.
Internal audit	An internal audit is an independent appraisal of operations, conducted under the direction of management, to assess the effectiveness of internal administrative and accounting controls and help ensure conformance with managerial policies.

Audit	Audit refers to the verification of a company's books and records pursuant to federal securities laws, state laws, and stock exchange rules that must be performed by an independent CPA.
Centralized authority	An organization structure in which decision-making authority is maintained at the top level of management at the company's headquarters is a centralized authority.
Commerce	Commerce is the exchange of something of value between two entities. It is the central mechanism from which capitalism is derived.
Client	The organizations with the products, services, or causes to be marketed and for which advertising agencies and other marketing promotional firms provide services is referred to as a client.
Certification audits	Audits relating to registration are called certification audits.
Compliance	A type of influence process where a receiver accepts the position advocated by a source to obtain favorable outcomes or to avoid punishment is the compliance.
Comprehensive	A comprehensive refers to a layout accurate in size, color, scheme, and other necessary details to show how a final ad will look. For presentation only, never for reproduction.
Environmental protection agency	An administrative agency created by Congress in 1970 to coordinate the implementation and enforcement of the federal environmental protection laws is referred to as the Environmental Protection Agency or EPA.
Agency	Agency refers to a legal relationship in which an agent acts under the direction of a principal for the principal's benefit. Also used to refer to government regulatory bodies of all kinds.
Adoption	In corporation law, a corporation's acceptance of a pre-incorporation contract by action of its board of directors, by which the corporation becomes liable on the contract, is referred to as adoption.
Premium	Premium refers to the fee charged by an insurance company for an insurance policy. The rate of losses must be relatively predictable: In order to set the premium (prices) insurers must be able to estimate them accurately.
Economic union	Economic union refers to a group of countries committed to removing all barriers to the free flow of goods, services, and factors of production between each other, the adoption of a common currency, the harmonization of tax rates, and the pursuit of a common external trade policy.
Union	A union refers to employee organizations that have the main goal of representing members in employeemanagement bargaining over job-related issues.
Unions	Employee organizations that have the main goal of representing members in employeemanagement bargaining over job-related issues are called unions.
Group technology	A component of CAD that allows for the cataloging and standardization of parts and components for complex products is a group technology.
Economy	The income, expenditures, and resources that affect the cost of running a business and household are called an economy.

Go to **Cram101.com** for the Practice Tests for this Chapter.

Quality measures	Ratios that are used to measure a firm's performance in the area of quality management are referred to as quality measures.
Strategic planning	The process of determining the major goals of the organization and the policies and strategies for obtaining and using resources to achieve those goals is called strategic planning.
Content	Content refers to all digital information included on a website, including the presentation form-text, video, audio, and graphics.
Strategic plan	The formal document that presents the ways and means by which a strategic goal will be achieved is a strategic plan. A long-term flexible plan that does not regulate activities but rather outlines the means to achieve certain results, and provides the means to alter the course of action should the desired ends change.
Yield	The interest rate that equates a future value or an annuity to a given present value is a yield.
Competency	Competency refers to a person's ability to understand the nature of the transaction and the consequences of entering into it at the time the contract was entered into.
Total Quality Management	The practice of striving for customer satisfaction by ensuring quality from all departments in an organization is called total quality management.
Quality management	Quality management is a method for ensuring that all the activities necessary to design, develop and implement a product or service are effective and efficient with respect to the system and its performance.
Management	Management characterizes the process of leading and directing all or part of an organization, often a business, through the deployment and manipulation of resources. Early twentieth-century management writer Mary Parker Follett defined management as "the art of getting things done through people."
Comprehensive	A comprehensive refers to a layout accurate in size, color, scheme, and other necessary details to show how a final ad will look. For presentation only, never for reproduction.
Accounting	The recording, classifying, summarizing, and interpreting of financial events and transactions to provide management and other interested parties the information they need to make good decisions is called accounting.
Industry	Industry refers to a group of firms offering products that are close substitutes for each other.
Competitor	Other organizations in the same industry or type of business that provide a good or service to the same set of customers is referred to as a competitor.
Market share	The ratio of sales revenue of the firm to the total sales revenue of all firms in the industry, including the firm itself is the market share.
Case study	A case study is a particular method of qualitative research. Rather than using large samples and following a rigid protocol to examine a limited number of variables, case study methods involve an in-depth, longitudinal examination of a single instance or event: a case. They provide a systematic way of looking at events, collecting data, analyzing information, and reporting the results.
Manager	A person who is formally responsible for supporting the work efforts of other people is a manager.
In-process inspection	The practice of inspecting work, by the workers themselves, at each stage of the production process is an in-process inspection.

Plan-do-check-act cycle	Plan-do-check-act cycle refers to a process for improvement pioneered by W. E. Deming. A cycle of activities designed to drive continuous improvement.
Organizational learning	Organizational learning is an area of knowledge within organizational theory that studies models and theories about the way an organization learns and adapts.
Budget	A financial plan that sets forth management's expectations for revenues and, based on those expectations, allocates the use of specific resources throughout the firm is called budget.
Authority	Authority in agency law, refers to an agent's ability to affect his principal's legal relations with third parties. Also used to refer to an actor's legal power or ability to do something. In addition, sometimes used to refer to a statute, case, or other legal source that justifies a particular result.
Superordinate goal	Superordinate goal refers to an organizational goal that is more important to the well-being of the organization and its members than the more specific goals of interacting parties.
Promotion	Promotion refers to all the techniques sellers use to motivate people to buy products or services. An attempt by marketers to inform people about products and to persuade them to participate in an exchange.
Incentive	A reward offered by a marketer to a prospective customer in return for furnishing information or making a purchase is referred to as an incentive.
Communism	An economic and political system in which the state makes all economic decisions and owns all the major forms of production is communism.
Coercive power	Coercive power refers to the extent to which a person has the ability to punish or physically or psychologically harm someone else.
Unions	Employee organizations that have the main goal of representing members in employeemanagement bargaining over job-related issues are called unions.
Union	A union refers to employee organizations that have the main goal of representing members in employeemanagement bargaining over job-related issues.
Referent power	Referent power is individual power based on a high level of identification with, admiration of, or respect for the powerholder.
Mentor	An experienced employee who supervises, coaches, and guides lower-level employees by introducing them to the right people and generally being their organizational sponsor is a mentor.
Legitimate power	Legitimate power refers to power that is granted by virtue of one's position in the organization.
Trait dimension	A view of leadership that states that leadership potential is related to the 'traits' of an individual, such as height is a trait dimension.
Exhibit	Exhibit refers to a copy of a written instrument on which a pleading is founded, annexed to the pleading and by reference made a part of it. Any paper or thing offered in evidence and marked for identification.
Communication	Communication refers to the social process in which two or more parties exchange information and share meaning.
Categorizing	The act of placing strengths and weaknesses into categories in generic internal assessment is called categorizing.
Trust	Trust refers to a legal relationship in which a person who has legal title to property has the duty to hold it for the use or benefit of another person. The term is also used in a general sense to mean confidence reposed in one person by another.

Go to **Cram101.com** for the Practice Tests for this Chapter.

Productivity	Productivity refers to the total output of goods and services in a given period of time divided by work hours.
Efficiency	Efficiency refers to the use of minimal resources, such as raw materials, money, and people- to produce a desired volume of output.
Corporation	A form of business organization that is owned by owners, called shareholders, who have no inherent right to manage the business, and is managed by a board of directors that is elected by the shareholders is called a corporation.
Policy	Similar to a script in that a policy can be a less than completely rational decision-making method. Involves the use of a pre-existing set of decision steps for any problem that presents itself.
Downsizing	The process of eliminating managerial and non-managerial positions are called downsizing.
Attrition	The practice of not hiring new employees to replace older employees who either quit or retire is referred to as attrition.
Forming	The first stage of team development, where the team is formed and the objectives for the team are set is referred to as forming.
Malcolm Baldrige National Quality Award	Malcolm Baldrige national quality award refers to U.S. national quality award sponsored by the U.S. Department of Commerce and private industry. The program aims to reward quality in the business sector, health care, and education, and was inspired by the ideas of Total Quality Management.
Customer service	The ability of logistics management to satisfy users in terms of time, dependability, communication, and convenience is called the customer service.
Budget cycle	The timed steps of the budget process, which includes preparation, approval, execution, and audit is the budget cycle.
Mission statement	Mission statement refers to an outline of the fundamental purposes of an organization.
Compensation	A payment that is given or recieved as reparation for a service or loss is referred to as compensation.
Empathy	Empathy refers to dimension of service quality-caring individualized attention provided to customers.
Economy	The income, expenditures, and resources that affect the cost of running a business and household are called an economy.
Product	Any physical good, service, or idea that satisfies a want or need is called product. Product in project management is a physical entity created as a result of project work.
Business model	A business model is the instrument by which a business intends to generate revenue and profits. It is a summary of how a company means to serve its employees and customers, and involves both strategy (what an business intends to do) as well as an implementation.
Production	The creation of finished goods and services using the factors of production: land, labor, capital, entrepreneurship, and knowledge.
Participation	Participation refers to the process of giving employees a voice in making decisions about their own work.
Exporting	Selling products to another country is called exporting.
Interest	Interest refers to the payment the issuer of the bond makes to the bondholders for use of the borrowed money. It is the return to capital achieved over time or as the result of an event.

Failure costs	Two sets of costs-internal failure costs and external failure costs are called failure costs. Internal failure costs include those costs that are associated with failure during production, whereas external failure costs are associated with product failure after the production process.
Direct costs	Direct costs are those costs that can be identified specifically with a particular sponsored project, an instructional activity, or any other institutional activity, or that can be directly assigned to such activities relatively easily with a high degree of accuracy.
Quality control	The measurement of products and services against set standards is referred to as quality control.
Appraisal costs	Expenses associated with the direct costs of measuring quality are called appraisal costs.
Assessment	Collecting information and providing feedback to employees about their behavior, communication style, or skills is an assessment.
Internal failure costs	Internal failure costs refers to losses that occur while the product is in possession of the producer. These include rework and scrap costs.
Internal failure cost	An internal failure cost refers to any loss that occurs while a product is in possession of the producer. These include rework and scrap costs.
External failure costs	External failure costs refer to monetary losses associated with product failures after the customer has possession of the product. These may include warranty or field repair costs.
Possession	Possession refers to respecting real property, exclusive dominion and control such as owners of like property usually exercise over it. Manual control of personal property either as owner or as one having a qualified right in it.
Law of diminishing marginal returns	A law that stipulates that there is a point at which investment in quality improvement will become uneconomical is a law of diminishing marginal returns.
Conformance	A dimension of quality that refers to the extent to which a product lies within an allowable range of deviation from its specification is called the conformance.
Continuous improvement	Constantly improving the way the organization does things so that customer needs can be better satisfied is referred to as continuous improvement.
Market price	The price determined by supply and demand is referred to as the market price.
Receiver	A person that is appointed as a custodian of other people's property by a court of law or a creditor of the owner, pending a lawsuit or reorganization is called a receiver.
Appeal	Appeal refers to the act of asking an appellate court to overturn a decision after the trial court's final judgment has been entered.
Stock	In financial terminology, stock is the capital raized by a corporation, through the issuance and sale of shares. A shareholder is any person or organization which owns one or more shares of a corporation's stock. The aggregate value of a corporation's issued shares is its market capitalization.
Client	The organizations with the products, services, or causes to be marketed and for which advertising agencies and other marketing promotional firms provide services is referred to as a client.
Advertising	Advertising refers to paid, nonpersonal communication through various media by organizations and individuals who are in some way identified in the advertising message.
Marketing	The American Marketing Association suggests that Marketing is "the process of planning and

executing the pricing, promotion, and distribution of goods, ideas, and services to create exchanges that satisfy individual and organizational goals."

Flexible manufacturing system	A smallor medium-sized automated production line that can be adapted to produce more than one product line is a flexible manufacturing system.
Flexible manufacturing	Flexible manufacturing refers to designing machines to do multiple tasks so that they can produce a variety of products.
Manufacturing	Manufacturing is the transformation of raw materials into finished goods for sale, by means of tools and a processing medium, and including all intermediate processes involving the production or finishing of component parts.
Core	A core is the set of feasible allocations in an economy that cannot be improved upon by subset of the set of the economy's consumers (a coalition).
Competencies	An organization's special capabilities, including skills, technologies, and resources that distinguish it from other organizations are competencies.
Asset	In business and accounting an asset is anything owned which can produce future economic benefit, whether in possession or by right to take possession, by a person or a group acting together, e.g. a company, the measurement of which can be expressed in monetary terms. Asset is listed on the balance sheet. It has a normal balance of debit.
Diversification	Diversification is a strategy that takes the organization away from both its current markets and products, as opposed to either market or product development.
Attractiveness	A source characteristic that makes him or her appealing to a message recipient is attractiveness. Source attractiveness can be based on similarity, familiarity, or likeability.
Management control	That aspect of management concerned with the comparison of actual versus planned performance as well as the development and implementation of procedures to correct substandard performance is called management control.
Basic seven tools of quality	Basic seven tools of quality refers to the fundamental methods for gathering and analyzing quality related data. They are: fishbone diagrams, histograms, Pareto analysis, flowcharts, scatter plots, run charts, and control charts.
Quality function deployment	Quality function deployment involves developing a matrix that includes customer preferences and product attributes. A quality function deployment matrix allows a firm to quantitatively analyze the relationship between customer needs and design attributes.
Hoshin planning process	A policy deployment approach to strategic planning originated by Japanese firms is referred to as hoshin planning process.
Corporate goals	Strategic performance targets that the entire organization must reach to pursue its vision are referred to as corporate goals.
Dumping	The selling of goods by a seller in a foreign nation at unfairly low prices is referred to as dumping.
Competition	In business, competition occurs when rival organizations with similar products and services attempt to gain customers.
Competitive advantage	A business is said to have a competitive advantage when its unique strengths, often based on cost, quality, time, and innovation, offer consumers a greater percieved value and there by differtiating it from its competitors.
Learning	A firm, which values continuous learning and is consistently looking to adapt and change with

organization	its environment is referred to as learning organization.
Administrator	Administrator refers to the personal representative appointed by a probate court to settle the estate of a deceased person who died.
Value analysis	Value analysis refers to a systematic appraisal of the design, quality, and performance of a product to reduce purchasing costs.
Regulation	Regulation refers to restrictions state and federal laws place on business with regard to the conduct of its activities.

48

Go to **Cram101.com** for the Practice Tests for this Chapter.

Customer service	The ability of logistics management to satisfy users in terms of time, dependability, communication, and convenience is called the customer service.
Product	Any physical good, service, or idea that satisfies a want or need is called product. Product in project management is a physical entity created as a result of project work.
Receiver	A person that is appointed as a custodian of other people's property by a court of law or a creditor of the owner, pending a lawsuit or reorganization is called a receiver.
External customers	Dealers, who buy products to sell to others, and ultimate customers, who buy products for their own personal use are referred to as external customers.
Internal customer	An individuals or unit within the firm that receives services from other entities within the organization is an internal customer.
Management	Management characterizes the process of leading and directing all or part of an organization, often a business, through the deployment and manipulation of resources. Early twentieth-century management writer Mary Parker Follett defined management as "the art of getting things done through people."
Information system	An information system is a system whether automated or manual, that comprises people, machines, and/or methods organized to collect, process, transmit, and disseminate data that represent user information.
Users	Users refer to people in the organization who actually use the product or service purchased by the buying center.
Accounting	The recording, classifying, summarizing, and interpreting of financial events and transactions to provide management and other interested parties the information they need to make good decisions is called accounting.
Internal service	A service that is provided by personnel from within the company is an internal service. For example, data processing personnel are often considered providers of an internal service.
End user	End user refers to the ultimate user of a product or service.
Malcolm Baldrige National Quality Award	Malcolm Baldrige national quality award refers to U.S. national quality award sponsored by the U.S. Department of Commerce and private industry. The program aims to reward quality in the business sector, health care, and education, and was inspired by the ideas of Total Quality Management.
Purchasing	Purchasing refers to the function in a firm that searches for quality material resources, finds the best suppliers, and negotiates the best price for goods and services.
Restructuring	Restructuring is the corporate management term for the act of partially dismantling and reorganizing a company for the purpose of making it more efficient and therefore more profitable.
Reactive customer-driven quality	A state that is characterized by a supplier 'reacting' to the quality expectations of a customer rather than proactively anticipating customer needs and expectations is called reactive customer-driven quality.
Competitor	Other organizations in the same industry or type of business that provide a good or service to the same set of customers is referred to as a competitor.
Competition	In business, competition occurs when rival organizations with similar products and services attempt to gain customers.
Voice of the customer	A term that refers to the wants, opinions, perceptions, and desires of the customer is a voice of the customer.
Production	The creation of finished goods and services using the factors of production: land, labor,

capital, entrepreneurship, and knowledge.

Quality function deployment	Quality function deployment involves developing a matrix that includes customer preferences and product attributes. A quality function deployment matrix allows a firm to quantitatively analyze the relationship between customer needs and design attributes.
Marketing	The American Marketing Association suggests that Marketing is "the process of planning and executing the pricing, promotion, and distribution of goods, ideas, and services to create exchanges that satisfy individual and organizational goals."
Budget	A financial plan that sets forth management's expectations for revenues and, based on those expectations, allocates the use of specific resources throughout the firm is called budget.
Direct marketing	Promotional element that uses direct communication with consumers to generate a response in the form of an order, a request for further information, or a visit to a retail outlet is direct marketing.
Relationship management	A method for developing long-term associations with customers is referred to as relationship management.
Tangibles	Dimension of service quality-appearance of physical facilities, equipment, personnel, and communication materials are called tangibles.
Tangible	Having a physical existence is referred to as the tangible. Personal property other than real estate, such as cars, boats, stocks, or other assets.
Empathy	Empathy refers to dimension of service quality-caring individualized attention provided to customers.
Customer-relationship management	Customer-relationship management refers to a view of the customer that asserts that the customer is a valued asset that should be managed.
Complaint	The pleading in a civil case in which the plaintiff states his claim and requests relief is called complaint. In the common law, it is a formal legal document that sets out the basic facts and legal reasons that the filing party (the plaintiffs) believes are sufficient to support a claim against another person, persons, entity or entities (the defendants) that entitles the plaintiff(s) to a remedy (either money damages or injunctive relief).
Quality management	Quality management is a method for ensuring that all the activities necessary to design, develop and implement a product or service are effective and efficient with respect to the system and its performance.
Corporation	A form of business organization that is owned by owners, called shareholders, who have no inherent right to manage the business, and is managed by a board of directors that is elected by the shareholders is called a corporation.
Expense	An expense refers to costs involved in operating a business, such as rent, utilities, and salaries.
Policy	Similar to a script in that a policy can be a less than completely rational decision-making method. Involves the use of a pre-existing set of decision steps for any problem that presents itself.
Complaint-recovery process	Process associated with resolving complaints is referred to as complaint-recovery process.
Channel	Channel, in communications (sometimes called communications channel), refers to the medium used to convey information from a sender (or transmitter) to a receiver.

Exchange	The trade of things of value between buyer and seller so that each is better off after the trade is called the exchange.
Conformance	A dimension of quality that refers to the extent to which a product lies within an allowable range of deviation from its specification is called the conformance.
Level of service	The degree of service provided to the customer by self, limited, and full-service retailers is referred to as the level of service.
Gap analysis	An evaluation tool that compares expectations about a service offering to the actual experience a consumer has with the service is a gap analysis.
Quality dimension	A quality dimension refers to aspects of quality that help to better define what quality is. These include perceived quality, conformance, reliability, durability, and so on.
Servqual	A survey instrument designed to assess service quality along five specific dimensions consisting of tangibles, reliability, responsiveness, assurance, and empathy is referred to as servqual.
Manager	A person who is formally responsible for supporting the work efforts of other people is a manager.
Context	The effect of the background under which a message often takes on more and richer meaning is a context. Context is especially important in cross-cultural interactions because some cultures are said to be high context or low context.
Industry	Industry refers to a group of firms offering products that are close substitutes for each other.
Demographics	Demographics is a shorthand term for 'population characteristics'. Demographics include race, age, income, mobility (in terms of travel time to work or number of vehicles available), educational attainment, home ownership, employment status, and even location. Demographics are primarily used in economic and marketing research.
Demographic	A demographic is a term used in marketing and broadcasting, to describe a demographic grouping or a market segment.
Contract	A contract is a "promise" or an "agreement" that is enforced or recognized by the law. In the civil law, contracts are considered to be part of the general law of obligations. This article describes the law relating to contracts in common law jurisdictions.
Just-in-time	Just In Time (JIT) is an inventory strategy implemented to improve the return on investment of a business by reducing in-process inventory and its associated costs.
De facto	De facto, in fact, actual. Often used in contrast to de jure to refer to a real state of affairs.
Productivity	Productivity refers to the total output of goods and services in a given period of time divided by work hours.
Complexity	The technical sophistication of the product and hence the amount of understanding required to use it is referred to as complexity. It is the opposite of simplicity.
Control system	A control system is a device or set of devices that manage the behavior of other devices. Some devices or systems are not controllable.A control system is an interconnection of components connected or related in such a manner as to command, direct, or regulate itself or another system.
Audit	Audit refers to the verification of a company's books and records pursuant to federal securities laws, state laws, and stock exchange rules that must be performed by an independent CPA.

Customer rationalization	The process of reaching an agreement between marketing and operations as to which customers add the greatest advantage and profits over time is referred to as customer rationalization.
Annuity relationship	Annuity relationship occurs when a business receives many repeat purchases from a customer. The income is received steadily over time from a single customer.
Annuity	A contract to make regular payments to a person for life or for a fixed period is an annuity.
Active data gathering	A method for gathering data that involves approaching respondents to get information is active data gathering.
Passive data gathering	Passive data gathering occurs when the customer initiates the data gathering for a firm such as filling out a customer complaint card or sending an e-mail. The firm provides the mechanism for feedback, the customer must initiate the use of the mechanism.
Soft data	Data that cannot be measured or specifically quantified, such as survey data that asks respondents to provide their 'opinion' about something is called soft data.
Customer contact	Customer contact refers to a characteristic of services that notes that customers tend to be more involved in the production of services than they are in manufactured goods.
Warranty	A warranty is a promise that something sold is as factually stated or legally implied by the seller. A warranty may be express or implied. A breach of warranty occurs when the promise is broken, i.e., a product is defective or not as should be expected by a reasonable buyer.
Interest	Interest refers to the payment the issuer of the bond makes to the bondholders for use of the borrowed money. It is the return to capital achieved over time or as the result of an event.
Focus group	A small group of people who meet under the direction of a discussion leader to communicate their opinions about an organization, its products, or other given issues is a focus group.
Market segments	Market segments refer to the groups that result from the process of market segmentation; these groups ideally have common needs and will respond similarly to a marketing action.
Assessment	Collecting information and providing feedback to employees about their behavior, communication style, or skills is an assessment.
Content	Content refers to all digital information included on a website, including the presentation form-text, video, audio, and graphics.
Pareto analysis	Pareto analysis is a statistical technique in decision making used for selection of a limited number of tasks that produce significant overall effect.
Variance	In budgeting a variance is a difference between budgeted, planned or standard amount and the actual amount incurred/sold.
Passively solicited customer feedback	Passively solicited customer feedback refers to a method of soliciting customer feedback that is left to the customer to initiate, such as filling out a restaurant complaint card or calling a toll-free complaint line.
Personnel	A collective term for all of the employees of an organization. Personnel is also commonly used to refer to the personnel management function or the organizational unit responsible for administering personnel programs.
Merchant	Under the Uniform Commercial Code, one who regularly deals in goods of the kind sold in the contract at issue, or holds himself out as having special knowledge or skill relevant to such goods, or who makes the sale through an agent who regularly deals in such goods or claims such knowledge or skill is referred to as merchant.
Customer retention	Customer retention refers to the percentage of customers who return to a service provider or continue to purchase a manufactured product.

Loyalty	Marketers tend to define customer loyalty as making repeat purchases. Some argue that it should be defined attitudinally as a strongly positive feeling about the brand.
Electronic data interchange	Combine proprietary computer and telecommunication technologies to exchange electronic invoices, payments, and information among suppliers, manufacturers, and retailers is referred to as the electronic data interchange.
Brand loyalty	The degree to which customers are satisfied, like the brand, and are committed to further purchase is referred to as brand loyalty.
Brand	A name, symbol, or design that identifies the goods or services of one seller or group of sellers and distinguishes them from the goods and services of competitors is a brand.
Logo	Logo refers to device or other brand name that cannot be spoken.
Acquisition	A company's purchase of the property and obligations of another company is an acquisition.
Information technology	Information technology refers to technology that helps companies change business by allowing them to use new methods.
Discount	A discount is the reduction of the base price of a product.
Configuration	An organization's shape, which reflects the division of labor and the means of coordinating the divided tasks is configuration.
Personalization	The consumer-initiated practice of generating content on a marketer's website that is custom tailored to an individual's specific needs and preferences is called personalization.
Supply-chain management	Supply-chain management refers to the process of managing the movement of raw materials, parts, work in progress, finished goods, and related information through all the organizations involved in the supply chain; managing the return of such goods, if necessary.
Ready-fire-aim	A method that focuses on getting new technology to market and then determining how to sell the products is called ready-fire-aim.
Hearing	A hearing is a proceeding before a court or other decision-making body or officer. A hearing is generally distinguished from a trial in that it is usually shorter and often less formal.

Estate	An estate is the totality of the legal rights, interests, entitlements and obligations attaching to property. In the context of wills and probate, it refers to the totality of the property which the deceased owned or in which some interest was held.
Customer service	The ability of logistics management to satisfy users in terms of time, dependability, communication, and convenience is called the customer service.
Competitor	Other organizations in the same industry or type of business that provide a good or service to the same set of customers is referred to as a competitor.
Interest	Interest refers to the payment the issuer of the bond makes to the bondholders for use of the borrowed money. It is the return to capital achieved over time or as the result of an event.
Targeting	Targeting refers to the ability to address personalized promotions to a particular person who may be identified or described by means of an anonymous profile.
Options	Options give the owner the right but not the obligation to buy or sell an underlying security at a set price for a given time period.
Product	Any physical good, service, or idea that satisfies a want or need is called product. Product in project management is a physical entity created as a result of project work.
Production	The creation of finished goods and services using the factors of production: land, labor, capital, entrepreneurship, and knowledge.
Productivity	Productivity refers to the total output of goods and services in a given period of time divided by work hours.
Competitive advantage	A business is said to have a competitive advantage when its unique strengths, often based on cost, quality, time, and innovation, offer consumers a greater percieved value and there by diffentiating it from its competitors.
Strategic alliance	Strategic alliance refers to a long-term partnership between two or more companies established to help each company build competitive market advantages.
Benchmarking	Discovering how others do something better than your own firm so you can imitate or leapfrog competition is called benchmarking.
Competition	In business, competition occurs when rival organizations with similar products and services attempt to gain customers.
Marketing	The American Marketing Association suggests that Marketing is "the process of planning and executing the pricing, promotion, and distribution of goods, ideas, and services to create exchanges that satisfy individual and organizational goals."
Industry	Industry refers to a group of firms offering products that are close substitutes for each other.
Manager	A person who is formally responsible for supporting the work efforts of other people is a manager.
Initiator firm	Initiator firm refers to the firm that is interested in benchmarking and initiates contact with benchmark firms.
Target firm	The firm that is being studied or benchmarked against is referred to as target firm.
Process benchmarking	A type of benchmarking that focuses on the observation of business processes including process flows, operating systems, process technologies, and the operation of target firms or departments is process benchmarking.
Best practice	In business management, a best practice is a generally accepted "best way of doing a thing". A best practice is formulated after the study of specific business or organizational case

Go to **Cram101.com** for the Practice Tests for this Chapter.

	studies to determine the most broadly effective and efficient means of organizing a system or performing a function.
Financial benchmarking	A type of benchmarking that typically involves using CD-ROM databases such as Lexis/Nexis or Compact Disclosure to gather information about competing firms to perform financial analyses and compare results is called financial benchmarking.
Quality measures	Ratios that are used to measure a firm's performance in the area of quality management are referred to as quality measures.
Accounting	The recording, classifying, summarizing, and interpreting of financial events and transactions to provide management and other interested parties the information they need to make good decisions is called accounting.
Product benchmarking	A type of benchmarking that firms employ when designing new products or upgrades to current products is product benchmarking.
Reverse engineering	Reverse engineering refers to the process of dismantling a competitor's products to understand the strengths and weaknesses of the designs.
Malcolm Baldrige National Quality Award	Malcolm Baldrige national quality award refers to U.S. national quality award sponsored by the U.S. Department of Commerce and private industry. The program aims to reward quality in the business sector, health care, and education, and was inspired by the ideas of Total Quality Management.
Deming prize	Japanese quality award for individuals and groups that have contributed to the field of quality control is called the deming prize.
Quality management	Quality management is a method for ensuring that all the activities necessary to design, develop and implement a product or service are effective and efficient with respect to the system and its performance.
Management	Management characterizes the process of leading and directing all or part of an organization, often a business, through the deployment and manipulation of resources. Early twentieth-century management writer Mary Parker Follett defined management as "the art of getting things done through people."
Strategic benchmarking	Strategic benchmarking refers to a type of benchmarking that involves observing how others compete. This type of benchmarking typically involves target firms that have been identified as 'world class'.
Functional benchmarking	A type of benchmarking that involves the sharing of information among firms that are interested in the same functional issues is called functional benchmarking.
Purchasing	Purchasing refers to the function in a firm that searches for quality material resources, finds the best suppliers, and negotiates the best price for goods and services.
Cost of goods sold	A measure of the cost of merchandise sold or cost of raw materials and supplies used for producing items for resale is called cost of goods sold.
Efficiency	Efficiency refers to the use of minimal resources, such as raw materials, money, and people- to produce a desired volume of output.
Productivity ratios	Productivity ratios refer to ratios that are used in measuring the extent to which a firm effectively uses its resources.
Asset	In business and accounting an asset is anything owned which can produce future economic benefit, whether in possession or by right to take possession, by a person or a group acting together, e.g. a company, the measurement of which can be expressed in monetary terms. Asset is listed on the balance sheet. It has a normal balance of debit.

Go to **Cram101.com** for the Practice Tests for this Chapter.

Policy	Similar to a script in that a policy can be a less than completely rational decision-making method. Involves the use of a pre-existing set of decision steps for any problem that presents itself.
Key business factors	Those measures or indicators that are significantly related to the business success of a particular firm are called key business factors.
Market share	The ratio of sales revenue of the firm to the total sales revenue of all firms in the industry, including the firm itself is the market share.
Financial ratio	A financial ratio is a ratio of two numbers of reported levels or flows of a company. It may be two financial flows categories divided by each other (profit margin, profit/revenue). It may be a level divided by a financial flow (price/earnings). It may be a flow divided by a level (return on equity or earnings/equity). The numerator or denominator may itself be a ratio (PEG ratio).
Income statement	Income statement refers to the financial statement that shows a firm's profit after costs, expenses, and taxes; it summarizes all of the resources that have come into the firm, all the resources that have left the firm, and the resulting net income.
Balance sheet	A balance sheet, in formal bookkeeping and accounting, is a statement of the book value of a business or other organization or person at a particular date, often at the end of its "fiscal year," as distinct from an income statement, also known as a profit and loss account (P&L), which records revenue and expenses over a specified period of time.
Customer perceived value	Customer perceived value refers to the valuation a customer attaches to a product or service based on assessment of its quality and usefulness. Quality + Utility ± Price = CPV.
Operating results	Operating results refers to measures that are important to monitoring and tracking the effectiveness of a company's operations.
Human resources	Human resources refers to the individuals within the firm, and to the portion of the firm's organization that deals with hiring, firing, training, and other personnel issues.
Consideration	Consideration in contract law, a basic requirement for an enforceable agreement under traditional contract principles, defined in this text as legal value, bargained for and given in exchange for an act or promise. In corporation law, cash or property contributed to a corporation in exchange for shares, or a promise to contribute such cash or property.
Comprehensive	A comprehensive refers to a layout accurate in size, color, scheme, and other necessary details to show how a final ad will look. For presentation only, never for reproduction.
Best in class	Term used to refer to firms or organizations that are viewed as the best in an industry on some meaningful criterion is referred to as best in class.
Best of the best	Term used to refer to outstanding world class benchmark firms is referred to as best of the best.
Business process	Business process refers to the individual activities of an enterprise. Processes can be viewed at a high level, for example, 'marketing,' or at the level of detailed subprocesses, for example, 'customer retention.'.
Context	The effect of the background under which a message often takes on more and richer meaning is a context. Context is especially important in cross-cultural interactions because some cultures are said to be high context or low context.
Conversion process	Aligning the inputs of a process together to form a product or service is referred to as conversion process.
Conversion	Conversion refers to any distinct act of dominion wrongfully exerted over another's personal property in denial of or inconsistent with his rights therein. That tort committed by a

person who deals with chattels not belonging to him in a manner that is inconsistent with the ownership of the lawful owner.

Control process	A process involving gathering processed data, analyzing processed data, and using this information to make adjustments to the process is a control process.
Control charts	Control charts refer to tools for monitoring process variation.
Control chart	The control chart, also known as the 'Shewhart chart' or 'process-behavior chart' is a statistical tool intended to assess the nature of variation in a process and to facilitate forecasting and management. The control chart is one of the seven basic tools of quality control, which include the histogram, Pareto chart, check sheet, control chart, cause-and-effect diagram, flowchart, and scatter diagram.
Feedback loop	Feedback loop consists of a response and feedback. It is a system where outputs are fed back into the system as inputs, increasing or decreasing effects.
Performance gap	This represents the difference in actual performance shown as compared to the desired standard of performance. In employee performance management efforts, this performance gap is often described in terms of needed knowledge and skills which become training and development goals for the employee.
Brainstorming	Brainstorming refers to a technique designed to overcome our natural tendency to evaluate and criticize ideas and thereby reduce the creative output of those ideas. People are encouraged to produce ideas/options without criticizing, often at a very fast pace to minimize our natural tendency to criticize.
Acceptance	The actual or implied receipt and retention of that which is tendered or offered is the acceptance.
Communication	Communication refers to the social process in which two or more parties exchange information and share meaning.
Operational goals	Specific, measurable results expected from departments, work groups, and individuals within the organization are called operational goals.
Personnel	A collective term for all of the employees of an organization. Personnel is also commonly used to refer to the personnel management function or the organizational unit responsible for administering personnel programs.
Stakeholder	Any individual or group that might be affected by the outcome of something. All decisions have their stakeholders. The responsible public decision maker seeks to obtain the maximum possible stakeholder satisfaction.
Competency	Competency refers to a person's ability to understand the nature of the transaction and the consequences of entering into it at the time the contract was entered into.
Protocol	Protocol refers to a statement that, before product development begins, identifies a well-defined target market; specific customers' needs, wants, and preferences; and what the product will be and do.
Organizational learning	Organizational learning is an area of knowledge within organizational theory that studies models and theories about the way an organization learns and adapts.
Reengineering	The fundamental rethinking and radical redesign of organizational processes to achieve dramatic improvements in critical measures of performance is reengineering.
Automation	Automation allows machines to do work previously accomplished by people.
Information technology	Information technology refers to technology that helps companies change business by allowing them to use new methods.

Process reengineering	Process reengineering refers to the total rethinking and redesign of organizational process to improve performance and innovation; involves analyzing, streamlining, and reconfiguring actions and tasks to achieve work goals.
Reciprocity	An industrial buying practice in which two organizations agree to purchase each other's products and services is called reciprocity.
Basic events	Term used in fault tree analysis. Basic events are initiating faults that do not require events below them to show how they occurred. The symbol used for a basic event is a circle.
Complexity	The technical sophistication of the product and hence the amount of understanding required to use it is referred to as complexity. It is the opposite of simplicity.
Probable cause	The reasonable inference from the available facts and circumstances that the suspect committed the crime is referred to as the probable cause.
Vendor	A person who sells property to a vendee is a vendor. The words vendor and vendee are more commonly applied to the seller and purchaser of real estate, and the words seller and buyer are more commonly applied to the seller and purchaser of personal property.
Product traceability	Product traceability refers to the ability to trace a component part of a product back to its original manufacturer.
Consumer	A consumer is a individual or household that consume goods and services generated within the economy. Since this includes just about everyone, the term is a political term as much as an economic term when it is used in everyday speech.
Product liability	Part of tort law that holds businesses liable for harm that results from the production, design, sale, or use of products they market is referred to as product liability.
Liability	A liability is anything that is a hindrance, or puts individuals at a disadvantage.
Green manufacturing	Green manufacturing refers to a method for manufacturing that minimizes waste and pollution. These goals are often achieved through product and process design.
Manufacturing	Manufacturing is the transformation of raw materials into finished goods for sale, by means of tools and a processing medium, and including all intermediate processes involving the production or finishing of component parts.
Design for reuse	Designing products so they can be used in later generations of products is referred to as design for reuse.
Design for disassembly	A method for developing products so that they can easily be taken apart is called design for disassembly.
Design for remanufacture	Design for remanufacture refers to a method for developing products so that the parts can be used in other products. Associated with green manufacturing.

Product	Any physical good, service, or idea that satisfies a want or need is called product. Product in project management is a physical entity created as a result of project work.
Quality assurance	Those activities associated with assuring the quality of a product or service is called quality assurance.
Quality dimension	A quality dimension refers to aspects of quality that help to better define what quality is. These include perceived quality, conformance, reliability, durability, and so on.
Marketing	The American Marketing Association suggests that Marketing is "the process of planning and executing the pricing, promotion, and distribution of goods, ideas, and services to create exchanges that satisfy individual and organizational goals."
Production	The creation of finished goods and services using the factors of production: land, labor, capital, entrepreneurship, and knowledge.
Corporation	A form of business organization that is owned by owners, called shareholders, who have no inherent right to manage the business, and is managed by a board of directors that is elected by the shareholders is called a corporation.
Idea generation	Developing a pool of concepts as candidates for new products is called idea generation.
Manager	A person who is formally responsible for supporting the work efforts of other people is a manager.
Management	Management characterizes the process of leading and directing all or part of an organization, often a business, through the deployment and manipulation of resources. Early twentieth-century management writer Mary Parker Follett defined management as "the art of getting things done through people."
Contract	A contract is a "promise" or an "agreement" that is enforced or recognized by the law. In the civil law, contracts are considered to be part of the general law of obligations. This article describes the law relating to contracts in common law jurisdictions.
Industry	Industry refers to a group of firms offering products that are close substitutes for each other.
Competitor	Other organizations in the same industry or type of business that provide a good or service to the same set of customers is referred to as a competitor.
Assessment	Collecting information and providing feedback to employees about their behavior, communication style, or skills is an assessment.
Technology feasibility statement	A feasibility statement used in the design process to assess a variety of issues such as necessary parameters for performance, manufacturing imperatives, limitations in the physics of materials, and conditions for quality testing the product is referred to as technology feasibility statement.
Distribution	Distribution is one of the four aspects of marketing. A distribution business is the middleman between the manufacturer and retailer or (usually)in commercial or industrial the business customer.
Preparation	Preparation refers to usually the first stage in the creative process. It includes education and formal training.
Marketing Plan	Marketing plan refers to a road map for the marketing activities of an organization for a specified future period of time, such as one year or five years.
Evaluation	The consumer's appraisal of the product or brand on important attributes is called evaluation.
Quality	Quality function deployment involves developing a matrix that includes customer preferences

function deployment	and product attributes. A quality function deployment matrix allows a firm to quantitatively analyze the relationship between customer needs and design attributes.
Voice of the customer	A term that refers to the wants, opinions, perceptions, and desires of the customer is a voice of the customer.
House of quality	A house of quality is developed during quality function deployment and shows the relationship of customer requirements to the means of achieving these requirements.
Focus group	A small group of people who meet under the direction of a discussion leader to communicate their opinions about an organization, its products, or other given issues is a focus group.
Competition	In business, competition occurs when rival organizations with similar products and services attempt to gain customers.
Computer-aided design	Computer-aided design is the use of a wide range of computer-based tools that assist engineers, architects and other design professionals in their design activities. It is the main geometry authoring tool within the Product Lifecycle Management process and involves both software and sometimes special-purpose hardware.
Multiuser	Multiuser is a term that defines an operating system that allows access of multiple users to the computer at the same time.
Multinational corporation	An organization that manufactures and markets products in many different countries and has multinational stock ownership and multinational management is referred to as multinational corporation.
Engineering analysis	Engineering analysis refers to the process of applying engineering concepts to the design of a product, including tests such as heat transfer analysis, stress analysis, or analysis of the dynamic behavior of the system being designed.
Design review	Design review is a formal, documented, comprehensive and systematic examination of a design to evaluate the design requirements and the capability of the design to meet the requirement for quality and to identify problems and propose solutions. A design review can be conducted at any stage of the design process.
Automation	Automation allows machines to do work previously accomplished by people.
Interference checking	A feasibility test for product designs to make sure that wires, cabling, and tubing in products such as airplanes don't conflict with each other is called interference checking.
Group technology	A component of CAD that allows for the cataloging and standardization of parts and components for complex products is a group technology.
Inventory	Inventory refers to physical material purchased from suppliers, which may or may not be reworked for sale to customers. A unique element of services-the need for and cost of having a service provider available.
Quality control	The measurement of products and services against set standards is referred to as quality control.
Control system	A control system is a device or set of devices that manage the behavior of other devices. Some devices or systems are not controllable.A control system is an interconnection of components connected or related in such a manner as to command, direct, or regulate itself or another system.
Prototyping	An iterative approach to design in which a series of mock-ups or models are developed until the customer and the designer come to agreement as to the final design is called prototyping.
Prototype	A prototype is built to test the function of a new design before starting production of a product.

Acceptance	The actual or implied receipt and retention of that which is tendered or offered is the acceptance.
Concurrent engineering	The simultaneous performance of product design and process design is concurrent engineering. Typically, concurrent engineering involves the formation of cross-functional teams. This allows engineers and managers of different disciplines to work together simultaneously in developing product and process designs.
Management team	A management team is directly responsible for managing the day-to-day operations (and profitability) of a company.
Communication	Communication refers to the social process in which two or more parties exchange information and share meaning.
Product Life Cycle	A theoretical model of what happens to sales and profits for a product over time is the product life cycle.
Complementary products	Products that use similar technologies and can coexist in a family of products are called complementary products. They tend to be purchased jointly and whose demands therefore are related.
Product line	A group of products that are physically similar or are intended for a similar market are called the product line.
Level production	Equal monthly production used to smooth out production schedules and employ manpower and equipment more efficiently and at a lower cost is referred to as level production.
Design for manufacture	Design for manufacture refers to the principle of designing products so that they are cost effective and easy to make.
Consideration	Consideration in contract law, a basic requirement for an enforceable agreement under traditional contract principles, defined in this text as legal value, bargained for and given in exchange for an act or promise. In corporation law, cash or property contributed to a corporation in exchange for shares, or a promise to contribute such cash or property.
Hierarchy	A system of grouping people in an organization according to rank from the top down in which all subordinate managers must report to one person is called a hierarchy.
Over-the-wall syndrome	Difficulties that arise when different types of engineers work in totally different departments in the same firm is called the over-the-wall syndrome.
Enterprise resource planning	Computer-based production and operations system that links multiple firms into one integrated production unit is enterprise resource planning.
Product data management	A method for gathering and evaluating product-related data is product data management. It is a category of computer software that aims to create an automatic link between CAD and a database, usually with data on what components something drawn using CAD consists of.
Extension	Extension refers to an out-of-court settlement in which creditors agree to allow the firm more time to meet its financial obligations. A new repayment schedule will be developed, subject to the acceptance of creditors.
Design phase	The phase in the instructional system design process where learning objectives, tests, and the required skills and knowledge for a task are constructed and sequenced is the design phase.
Discount	A discount is the reduction of the base price of a product.
Design for maintainability	A concept that states that products should be designed in a way that makes them easy for consumers to maintain is called design for maintainability.

Bottom line	Bottom line refers to the last line in a profit and loss statement; it refers to net profit.
Preventive maintenance	Maintaining scheduled upkeep and improvement to equipment so equipment can actually improve with age is called the preventive maintenance.
Component reliability	The propensity for a part to fail over a given time is referred to as component reliability.
Failure modes and effects analysis	Method for systematically considering each component of a system by identifying, analyzing, and documenting the possible failure modes within a system and the effects of each failure on the system is a failure modes and effects analysis.
Personnel	A collective term for all of the employees of an organization. Personnel is also commonly used to refer to the personnel management function or the organizational unit responsible for administering personnel programs.
Six Sigma	A means to 'delight the customer' by achieving quality through a highly disciplined process to focus on developing and delivering near-perfect products and services is called six sigma. Originally, it was defined as a metric for measuring defects and improving quality; and a methodology to reduce defect levels below 3.4 Defects Per (one) Million Opportunities (DPMO).
Mass production	The process of making a large number of a limited variety of products at very low cost is referred to as mass production.

76

Go to **Cram101.com** for the Practice Tests for this Chapter.

Conformance	A dimension of quality that refers to the extent to which a product lies within an allowable range of deviation from its specification is called the conformance.
Economy	The income, expenditures, and resources that affect the cost of running a business and household are called an economy.
Competitor	Other organizations in the same industry or type of business that provide a good or service to the same set of customers is referred to as a competitor.
Revenue	Revenue refers to the total amount of money a business earns in a given period by selling goods and services. The value of what is received for goods sold, services rendered.
Industry	Industry refers to a group of firms offering products that are close substitutes for each other.
Servqual	A survey instrument designed to assess service quality along five specific dimensions consisting of tangibles, reliability, responsiveness, assurance, and empathy is referred to as servqual.
Gap analysis	An evaluation tool that compares expectations about a service offering to the actual experience a consumer has with the service is a gap analysis.
Contingency perspective	Contingency perspective suggests that, in most organizations, situations and outcomes are contingent on, or influenced by, other variables.
Stock	In financial terminology, stock is the capital raized by a corporation, through the issuance and sale of shares. A shareholder is any person or organization which owns one or more shares of a corporation's stock. The aggregate value of a corporation's issued shares is its market capitalization.
Tangible	Having a physical existence is referred to as the tangible. Personal property other than real estate, such as cars, boats, stocks, or other assets.
Advertising	Advertising refers to paid, nonpersonal communication through various media by organizations and individuals who are in some way identified in the advertising message.
Production	The creation of finished goods and services using the factors of production: land, labor, capital, entrepreneurship, and knowledge.
Customer contact	Customer contact refers to a characteristic of services that notes that customers tend to be more involved in the production of services than they are in manufactured goods.
Customer coproduction	Customer coproduction refers to the participation of a customer in the delivery of a service product.
Product	Any physical good, service, or idea that satisfies a want or need is called product. Product in project management is a physical entity created as a result of project work.
External services	Service that are provided by companies other than yours is called external services.
Internal service	A service that is provided by personnel from within the company is an internal service. For example, data processing personnel are often considered providers of an internal service.
Data processing	Data processing refers to a name for business technology in the 1970s; included technology that supported an existing business and was primarily used to improve the flow of financial information.
Customer service	The ability of logistics management to satisfy users in terms of time, dependability, communication, and convenience is called the customer service.
Internal	An individuals or unit within the firm that receives services from other entities within the

customer	organization is an internal customer.
Accord	An agreement whereby the parties agree to accept something different in satisfaction of the original contract is an accord.
Intangibility	A unique element of services-services cannot be held, touched, or seen before the purchase decision which is referred to as intangibility.
Quality control	The measurement of products and services against set standards is referred to as quality control.
Control charts	Control charts refer to tools for monitoring process variation.
Control chart	The control chart, also known as the 'Shewhart chart' or 'process-behavior chart' is a statistical tool intended to assess the nature of variation in a process and to facilitate forecasting and management. The control chart is one of the seven basic tools of quality control, which include the histogram, Pareto chart, check sheet, control chart, cause-and-effect diagram, flowchart, and scatter diagram.
Warranty	A warranty is a promise that something sold is as factually stated or legally implied by the seller. A warranty may be express or implied. A breach of warranty occurs when the promise is broken, i.e., a product is defective or not as should be expected by a reasonable buyer.
Adoption	In corporation law, a corporation's acceptance of a pre-incorporation contract by action of its board of directors, by which the corporation becomes liable on the contract, is referred to as adoption.
Consideration	Consideration in contract law, a basic requirement for an enforceable agreement under traditional contract principles, defined in this text as legal value, bargained for and given in exchange for an act or promise. In corporation law, cash or property contributed to a corporation in exchange for shares, or a promise to contribute such cash or property.
Preparation	Preparation refers to usually the first stage in the creative process. It includes education and formal training.
Level of service	The degree of service provided to the customer by self, limited, and full-service retailers is referred to as the level of service.
Corporation	A form of business organization that is owned by owners, called shareholders, who have no inherent right to manage the business, and is managed by a board of directors that is elected by the shareholders is called a corporation.
Management	Management characterizes the process of leading and directing all or part of an organization, often a business, through the deployment and manipulation of resources. Early twentieth-century management writer Mary Parker Follett defined management as "the art of getting things done through people."
Manager	A person who is formally responsible for supporting the work efforts of other people is a manager.
Gold standard	The practice of pegging currencies to gold and guaranteeing convertibility is referred to as the gold standard.
Quality dimension	A quality dimension refers to aspects of quality that help to better define what quality is. These include perceived quality, conformance, reliability, durability, and so on.
Tangibles	Dimension of service quality-appearance of physical facilities, equipment, personnel, and communication materials are called tangibles.
Communication	Communication refers to the social process in which two or more parties exchange information and share meaning.

Contact personnel	The people at the 'front lines' who interact with the public in a service setting are contact personnel.
Personnel	A collective term for all of the employees of an organization. Personnel is also commonly used to refer to the personnel management function or the organizational unit responsible for administering personnel programs.
Word of mouth	People influencing each other during their face-to-face converzations is called word of mouth.
Closing	The finalization of a real estate sales transaction that passes title to the property from the seller to the buyer is referred to as a closing. Closing is a sales term which refers to the process of making a sale. It refers to reaching the final step, which may be an exchange of money or acquiring a signature.
Mistake	In contract law a mistake is incorrect understanding by one or more parties to a contract and may be used as grounds to invalidate the agreement. Common law has identified three different types of mistake in contract: unilateral mistake, mutual mistake, and common mistake.
Visibility	Visibility is used in marketing, as a measure of how much the public sees a product or its advertising.
Brainstorming	Brainstorming refers to a technique designed to overcome our natural tendency to evaluate and criticize ideas and thereby reduce the creative output of those ideas. People are encouraged to produce ideas/options without criticizing, often at a very fast pace to minimize our natural tendency to criticize.
Product Life Cycle	A theoretical model of what happens to sales and profits for a product over time is the product life cycle.
Confirmed	When the seller's bank agrees to assume liability on the letter of credit issued by the buyer's bank the transaction is confirmed. The term means that the credit is not only backed up by the issuing foreign bank, but that payment is also guaranteed by the notifying American bank.
Cabinet	The heads of the executive departments of a jurisdiction who report to and advise its chief executive; examples would include the president's cabinet, the governor's cabinet, and the mayor's cabinet.
Customer benefits package	The package of tangibles and intangibles that make up a service is called the customer benefits package.
Globalization	Trend away from distinct national economic units and toward one huge global market is called globalization. Globalization is caused by four fundamental forms of capital movement throughout the global economy.
Competition	In business, competition occurs when rival organizations with similar products and services attempt to gain customers.
Productivity	Productivity refers to the total output of goods and services in a given period of time divided by work hours.
Quality management	Quality management is a method for ensuring that all the activities necessary to design, develop and implement a product or service are effective and efficient with respect to the system and its performance.
Executive order	A legal rule issued by a chief executive usually pursuant to a delegation of power from the legislature is called executive order.
Early adopters	Early adopters refers to the 13.5 percent of the population who are leaders in their social

setting and act as an information source on new products for other people.

Social security	The term used to describe the Old-Age, Survivors, and Disability Insurance Program established by the Social Security Act of 1935 is social security.
Administration	Administration refers to the management and direction of the affairs of governments and institutions; a collective term for all policymaking officials of a government; the execution and implementation of public policy.
Strategic plan	The formal document that presents the ways and means by which a strategic goal will be achieved is a strategic plan. A long-term flexible plan that does not regulate activities but rather outlines the means to achieve certain results, and provides the means to alter the course of action should the desired ends change.
Privatization	A process in which investment bankers take companies that were previously owned by the government to the public markets is referred to as privatization.
Health maintenance organization	A Health Maintenance Organization is a fixed, prepaid health care plan that provides comprehensive benefits for employees who are required to use a network of participating providers for all health services.
Status quo	The existing state of things is the status quo. In contract law, returning a party to status quo or status quo ante means putting him in the position he was in before entering the contract.
Efficiency	Efficiency refers to the use of minimal resources, such as raw materials, money, and people-to produce a desired volume of output.
Empathy	Empathy refers to dimension of service quality-caring individualized attention provided to customers.
Corporate policy	Dimension of social responsibility that refers to the position a firm takes on social and political issues is referred to as corporate policy.
Policy	Similar to a script in that a policy can be a less than completely rational decision-making method. Involves the use of a pre-existing set of decision steps for any problem that presents itself.
Statistical thinking	Deming's concept relating to databased decision-making is statistical thinking. Statistical thinking is the tendency to want to understand complete situational understanding over a wide range of data where several control factors may be interacting at once to produce and outcome.
Bottom line	Bottom line refers to the last line in a profit and loss statement; it refers to net profit.

Corporation	A form of business organization that is owned by owners, called shareholders, who have no inherent right to manage the business, and is managed by a board of directors that is elected by the shareholders is called a corporation.
Accounting	The recording, classifying, summarizing, and interpreting of financial events and transactions to provide management and other interested parties the information they need to make good decisions is called accounting.
Purchasing	Purchasing refers to the function in a firm that searches for quality material resources, finds the best suppliers, and negotiates the best price for goods and services.
Logistics	Those activities that focus on getting the right amount of the right products to the right place at the right time at the lowest possible cost is referred to as logistics.
Quality control	The measurement of products and services against set standards is referred to as quality control.
Supply chain	The sequence of linked activities that must be performed by various organizations to move goods from the sources of raw materials to ultimate consumers is referred to as supply chain.
Value chain	A tool, developed by Michael Porter that decomposes a firm into its core activities is called value chain. The value chain categorizes the generic value-adding activities of an organization. The "primary activities" include: inbound logistics, operations (production), outbound logistics, sales and marketing, and service (maintenance).
Value system	A value system refers to how an individual or a group of individuals organize their ethical or ideological values. A well-defined value system is a moral code.
Outbound	Communications originating inside an organization and destined for customers, prospects, or other people outside the organization are called outbound.
Marketing	The American Marketing Association suggests that Marketing is "the process of planning and executing the pricing, promotion, and distribution of goods, ideas, and services to create exchanges that satisfy individual and organizational goals."
Chain of customers	A philosophy that espouses the idea that each worker's 'customer' is the next worker in the chain of people that produce a finished product or service is a chain of customers.
Product	Any physical good, service, or idea that satisfies a want or need is called product. Product in project management is a physical entity created as a result of project work.
Supply-chain management	Supply-chain management refers to the process of managing the movement of raw materials, parts, work in progress, finished goods, and related information through all the organizations involved in the supply chain; managing the return of such goods, if necessary.
Management	Management characterizes the process of leading and directing all or part of an organization, often a business, through the deployment and manipulation of resources. Early twentieth-century management writer Mary Parker Follett defined management as "the art of getting things done through people."
Distribution	Distribution is one of the four aspects of marketing. A distribution business is the middleman between the manufacturer and retailer or (usually)in commercial or industrial the business customer.
Extension	Extension refers to an out-of-court settlement in which creditors agree to allow the firm more time to meet its financial obligations. A new repayment schedule will be developed, subject to the acceptance of creditors.
Supplier partnering	Supplier partnering is the collaboration of a firm and its suppliers to boost quality, reduce cost, and to streamline production systems by establishing long term relationships where risk and reward are shared equally between the organizations.

Go to **Cram101.com** for the Practice Tests for this Chapter.

Just-in-time	Just In Time (JIT) is an inventory strategy implemented to improve the return on investment of a business by reducing in-process inventory and its associated costs.
Industry	Industry refers to a group of firms offering products that are close substitutes for each other.
De facto	De facto, in fact, actual. Often used in contrast to de jure to refer to a real state of affairs.
Single sourcing	Single sourcing is the origination of any design, set of concepts, or any article real or insubstantial from a single, well defined source, either a person or an organization.
Dual sourcing	Having two suppliers for the same product or service to ensure a continuous supply at a favorable price is referred to as dual sourcing.
Evaluation	The consumer's appraisal of the product or brand on important attributes is called evaluation.
External validation	External validation refers to using benchmarking as a way to ensure that a firm's current practices are comparable to those being used by benchmark firms.
Supplier development program	Provided by firms to their suppliers, a supplier development program is a training and development program that will improve the speed, quality, and cost of product delivery.
Audit	Audit refers to the verification of a company's books and records pursuant to federal securities laws, state laws, and stock exchange rules that must be performed by an independent CPA.
Unions	Employee organizations that have the main goal of representing members in employeemanagement bargaining over job-related issues are called unions.
Union	A union refers to employee organizations that have the main goal of representing members in employeemanagement bargaining over job-related issues.
Production	The creation of finished goods and services using the factors of production: land, labor, capital, entrepreneurship, and knowledge.
Communication	Communication refers to the social process in which two or more parties exchange information and share meaning.
Information system	An information system is a system whether automated or manual, that comprises people, machines, and/or methods organized to collect, process, transmit, and disseminate data that represent user information.
Electronic data interchange	Combine proprietary computer and telecommunication technologies to exchange electronic invoices, payments, and information among suppliers, manufacturers, and retailers is referred to as the electronic data interchange.
Inventory	Inventory refers to physical material purchased from suppliers, which may or may not be reworked for sale to customers. A unique element of services-the need for and cost of having a service provider available.
Materials management	Materials management refers to the activity that controls the transmission of physical materials through the value chain, from procurement through production and into distribution.
Statistical process control	Statistical process control is a method for achieving quality control in manufacturing processes. It is a set of methods using statistical tools such as mean, variance and others, to detect whether the process observed is under control.
Contract	A contract is a "promise" or an "agreement" that is enforced or recognized by the law. In the civil law, contracts are considered to be part of the general law of obligations. This

article describes the law relating to contracts in common law jurisdictions.

Administration	Administration refers to the management and direction of the affairs of governments and institutions; a collective term for all policymaking officials of a government; the execution and implementation of public policy.
Contingency perspective	Contingency perspective suggests that, in most organizations, situations and outcomes are contingent on, or influenced by, other variables.
QS 9000	A supplier development program developed by a Daimler Chrysler/Ford/General Motors supplier requirement task force is the QS 9000. The purpose of the QS 9000 is to provide a common standard and a set of procedures for the suppliers of the three companies.
TS 16949	TS 16949 refers to the ISO standard for supplier development and management replacing QS 9000 as an automotive industry standard.
Task force	A temporary team or committee formed to solve a specific short-term problem involving several departments is the task force.
Contribution	In business organization law, the cash or property contributed to a business by its owners is referred to as contribution.
Policy	Similar to a script in that a policy can be a less than completely rational decision-making method. Involves the use of a pre-existing set of decision steps for any problem that presents itself.
Authority	Authority in agency law, refers to an agent's ability to affect his principal's legal relations with third parties. Also used to refer to an actor's legal power or ability to do something. In addition, sometimes used to refer to a statute, case, or other legal source that justifies a particular result.
Personnel	A collective term for all of the employees of an organization. Personnel is also commonly used to refer to the personnel management function or the organizational unit responsible for administering personnel programs.
Liaison	An individual who serves as a bridge between groups, tying groups together and facilitating the communication flow needed to integrate group activities is a liaison.
Prototyping	An iterative approach to design in which a series of mock-ups or models are developed until the customer and the designer come to agreement as to the final design is called prototyping.
Contract review	Contract review involves the steps associated with contracting with suppliers. These steps involve acceptance of the contract or order, the tender of a contract, and review of the contract.
Acceptance	The actual or implied receipt and retention of that which is tendered or offered is the acceptance.
Tender	An unconditional offer of payment, consisting in the actual production in money or legal tender of a sum not less than the amount due.
Design control	A set of steps focused on managing the design of a product is referred to as design control.
Controlling	A management function that involves determining whether or not an organization is progressing toward its goals and objectives, and taking corrective action if it is not is called controlling.
Taguchi	Taguchi is an engineer and statistician who developed a methodology for applying statistics to improve the quality of manufactured goods. Taguchi methods have been controversial among many conventional Western statisticians.
Design review	Design review is a formal, documented, comprehensive and systematic examination of a design

to evaluate the design requirements and the capability of the design to meet the requirement for quality and to identify problems and propose solutions. A design review can be conducted at any stage of the design process.

Verification	Verification refers to the final stage of the creative process where the validity or truthfulness of the insight is determined. The feedback portion of communication in which the receiver sends a message to the source indicating receipt of the message and the degree to which he or she understood the message.
Product traceability	Product traceability refers to the ability to trace a component part of a product back to its original manufacturer.
Acceptance sampling	Acceptance sampling refers to an inspection of a sample from a lot to decide whether to accept or not accept that lot.
In-process inspection	The practice of inspecting work, by the workers themselves, at each stage of the production process is an in-process inspection.
Stock	In financial terminology, stock is the capital raized by a corporation, through the issuance and sale of shares. A shareholder is any person or organization which owns one or more shares of a corporation's stock. The aggregate value of a corporation's issued shares is its market capitalization.
Line authority	A form of authority in which individuals in management positions have the formal power to direct and control immediate subordinates is referred to as line authority.
Acceptable quality level	The maximum percentage or proportion of nonconformities in a lot or batch that can be considered satisfactory as a process average is an acceptable quality level.
Users	Users refer to people in the organization who actually use the product or service purchased by the buying center.
Consumer's risk	The risk of receiving a shipment of poor quality product and believing that it is good quality is referred to as consumer's risk.
Assignment	A transfer of property or some right or interest is referred to as assignment.
Sampling plan	In market research, the determination of how the data is to be collected, the interval of data collection, and the subjects from whom the data will be collected is called a sampling plan.
Bottom line	Bottom line refers to the last line in a profit and loss statement; it refers to net profit.
Assessment	Collecting information and providing feedback to employees about their behavior, communication style, or skills is an assessment.
Holding	The holding is a court's determination of a matter of law based on the issue presented in the particular case. In other words: under this law, with these facts, this result.
Front end	All the promotional activities that occur before a sale is made is a front end.

Quality management	Quality management is a method for ensuring that all the activities necessary to design, develop and implement a product or service are effective and efficient with respect to the system and its performance.
Management	Management characterizes the process of leading and directing all or part of an organization, often a business, through the deployment and manipulation of resources. Early twentieth-century management writer Mary Parker Follett defined management as "the art of getting things done through people."
Marketing	The American Marketing Association suggests that Marketing is "the process of planning and executing the pricing, promotion, and distribution of goods, ideas, and services to create exchanges that satisfy individual and organizational goals."
Accounting	The recording, classifying, summarizing, and interpreting of financial events and transactions to provide management and other interested parties the information they need to make good decisions is called accounting.
Human resources	Human resources refers to the individuals within the firm, and to the portion of the firm's organization that deals with hiring, firing, training, and other personnel issues.
Customer retention	Customer retention refers to the percentage of customers who return to a service provider or continue to purchase a manufactured product.
Business model	A business model is the instrument by which a business intends to generate revenue and profits. It is a summary of how a company means to serve its employees and customers, and involves both strategy (what an business intends to do) as well as an implementation.
Manager	A person who is formally responsible for supporting the work efforts of other people is a manager.
Reengineering	The fundamental rethinking and radical redesign of organizational processes to achieve dramatic improvements in critical measures of performance is reengineering.
Asset	In business and accounting an asset is anything owned which can produce future economic benefit, whether in possession or by right to take possession, by a person or a group acting together, e.g. a company, the measurement of which can be expressed in monetary terms. Asset is listed on the balance sheet. It has a normal balance of debit.
Innovation	The process of creating and doing new things that are introduced into the marketplace as products, processes, or services is innovation.
Production	The creation of finished goods and services using the factors of production: land, labor, capital, entrepreneurship, and knowledge.
Continuous improvement	Constantly improving the way the organization does things so that customer needs can be better satisfied is referred to as continuous improvement.
Basic seven tools of quality	Basic seven tools of quality refers to the fundamental methods for gathering and analyzing quality related data. They are: fishbone diagrams, histograms, Pareto analysis, flowcharts, scatter plots, run charts, and control charts.
Control charts	Control charts refer to tools for monitoring process variation.
Control chart	The control chart, also known as the 'Shewhart chart' or 'process-behavior chart' is a statistical tool intended to assess the nature of variation in a process and to facilitate forecasting and management. The control chart is one of the seven basic tools of quality control, which include the histogram, Pareto chart, check sheet, control chart, cause-and-effect diagram, flowchart, and scatter diagram.
Pareto analysis	Pareto analysis is a statistical technique in decision making used for selection of a limited number of tasks that produce significant overall effect.

Flowchart	A pictorial representation of the progression of a particular process over time is called a flowchart. They are commonly used in business/economic presentations to help the audience visualize the content better, or to find flaws in the process
Possession	Possession refers to respecting real property, exclusive dominion and control such as owners of like property usually exercise over it. Manual control of personal property either as owner or as one having a qualified right in it.
Authority	Authority in agency law, refers to an agent's ability to affect his principal's legal relations with third parties. Also used to refer to an actor's legal power or ability to do something. In addition, sometimes used to refer to a statute, case, or other legal source that justifies a particular result.
Forming	The first stage of team development, where the team is formed and the objectives for the team are set is referred to as forming.
Pareto chart	Chart used to identify and prioritize problems to be solved is a pareto chart. It is a special type of bar chart where the values being plotted are arranged in descending order.
Check sheet	A data-gathering tool that can be used in forming histograms is a check sheet. The check sheet can be either tabular or schematic.
Histogram	A representation of data in a bar chart format is called histogram.
Scatter diagram	A scatter plot used to examine the relationships between variables is called scatter diagram.
Conformance	A dimension of quality that refers to the extent to which a product lies within an allowable range of deviation from its specification is called the conformance.
Product	Any physical good, service, or idea that satisfies a want or need is called product. Product in project management is a physical entity created as a result of project work.
Facilitator	A facilitator is someone who skilfully helps a group of people understand their common objectives and plan to achieve them without personally taking any side of the argument.
Brainstorming	Brainstorming refers to a technique designed to overcome our natural tendency to evaluate and criticize ideas and thereby reduce the creative output of those ideas. People are encouraged to produce ideas/options without criticizing, often at a very fast pace to minimize our natural tendency to criticize.
Stock	In financial terminology, stock is the capital raized by a corporation, through the issuance and sale of shares. A shareholder is any person or organization which owns one or more shares of a corporation's stock. The aggregate value of a corporation's issued shares is its market capitalization.
Inventory	Inventory refers to physical material purchased from suppliers, which may or may not be reworked for sale to customers. A unique element of services-the need for and cost of having a service provider available.
Revenue	Revenue refers to the total amount of money a business earns in a given period by selling goods and services. The value of what is received for goods sold, services rendered.
Law of diminishing marginal returns	A law that stipulates that there is a point at which investment in quality improvement will become uneconomical is a law of diminishing marginal returns.
Committee	A long-lasting, sometimes permanent team in the organization structure created to deal with tasks that recur regularly is the committee.
Affinity diagram	A tool that is used to help groups identify the common themes that are associated with a

particular problem is referred to as affinity diagram.

Hierarchy	A system of grouping people in an organization according to rank from the top down in which all subordinate managers must report to one person is called a hierarchy.
Personnel	A collective term for all of the employees of an organization. Personnel is also commonly used to refer to the personnel management function or the organizational unit responsible for administering personnel programs.
Mission statement	Mission statement refers to an outline of the fundamental purposes of an organization.
Interrelatio- ship digraph	A visual display that maps out the cause and effect links among complex, multivariable problems or desired outcomes is an interrelationship digraph.
Consideration	Consideration in contract law, a basic requirement for an enforceable agreement under traditional contract principles, defined in this text as legal value, bargained for and given in exchange for an act or promise. In corporation law, cash or property contributed to a corporation in exchange for shares, or a promise to contribute such cash or property.
Options	Options give the owner the right but not the obligation to buy or sell an underlying security at a set price for a given time period.
Matrix diagram	A brainstorming tool that can be used in a group to show the relationships between ideas or issues is a matrix diagram.
Quality function deployment	Quality function deployment involves developing a matrix that includes customer preferences and product attributes. A quality function deployment matrix allows a firm to quantitatively analyze the relationship between customer needs and design attributes.
Layout	Layout refers to the physical arrangement of the various parts of an advertisement including the headline, subheads, illustrations, body copy, and any identifying marks.
Process decision program chart	Process decision program chart refers to a tool that is used to help brainstorm possible contingencies or problems associated with the implementation of some program or improvement.
Activity network diagram	An activity network diagram is a method for analyzing the tasks involved in completing a given project, especially the time needed to complete each task, and identifying the minimum time needed to complete the total project.
Program Evaluation and Review Technique	Program evaluation and review technique refers to a method for analyzing the tasks involved in completing a given project, estimating the time needed to complete each task, and identifying the minimum time needed to complete the total project.
Evaluation	The consumer's appraisal of the product or brand on important attributes is called evaluation.
Controlling	A management function that involves determining whether or not an organization is progressing toward its goals and objectives, and taking corrective action if it is not is called controlling.
Context	The effect of the background under which a message often takes on more and richer meaning is a context. Context is especially important in cross-cultural interactions because some cultures are said to be high context or low context.

Participation	Participation refers to the process of giving employees a voice in making decisions about their own work.
Teamwork	That which occurs when group members work together in ways that utilize their skills well to accomplish a purpose is called teamwork.
Complexity	The technical sophistication of the product and hence the amount of understanding required to use it is referred to as complexity. It is the opposite of simplicity.
Manager	A person who is formally responsible for supporting the work efforts of other people is a manager.
Collaboration	Collaboration occurs when the interaction between groups is very important to goal attainment and the goals are compatible. Wherein people work together —applying both to the work of individuals as well as larger collectives and societies.
Authority	Authority in agency law, refers to an agent's ability to affect his principal's legal relations with third parties. Also used to refer to an actor's legal power or ability to do something. In addition, sometimes used to refer to a statute, case, or other legal source that justifies a particular result.
Controlling	A management function that involves determining whether or not an organization is progressing toward its goals and objectives, and taking corrective action if it is not is called controlling.
Management	Management characterizes the process of leading and directing all or part of an organization, often a business, through the deployment and manipulation of resources. Early twentieth-century management writer Mary Parker Follett defined management as "the art of getting things done through people."
Loyalty	Marketers tend to define customer loyalty as making repeat purchases. Some argue that it should be defined attitudinally as a strongly positive feeling about the brand.
Incentive	A reward offered by a marketer to a prospective customer in return for furnishing information or making a purchase is referred to as an incentive.
Accountability	The extent to which one must answer to higher authority-legal or organizational-for one's actions in society at large or within one's particular organizational position is an accountability.
Empowerment	Giving employees the authority and responsibility to respond quickly to customer requests is called empowerment.
Consideration	Consideration in contract law, a basic requirement for an enforceable agreement under traditional contract principles, defined in this text as legal value, bargained for and given in exchange for an act or promise. In corporation law, cash or property contributed to a corporation in exchange for shares, or a promise to contribute such cash or property.
Trust	Trust refers to a legal relationship in which a person who has legal title to property has the duty to hold it for the use or benefit of another person. The term is also used in a general sense to mean confidence reposed in one person by another.
Job rotation	A job enrichment strategy that involves moving employees from one job to another is a job rotation.
Human resources	Human resources refers to the individuals within the firm, and to the portion of the firm's organization that deals with hiring, firing, training, and other personnel issues.
Alignment	Term that refers to optimal coordination among disparate departments and divisions within a firm is referred to as alignment.

Human resource management	The process of evaluating human resource needs, finding people to fill those needs, and getting the best work from each employee by providing the right incentives and job environment, all with the goal of meeting the needs of the firm are called human resource management.
Resource management	Resource management is the efficient and effective deployment of an organization's resources when they are needed. Such resources may include financial resources, inventory, human skills, production resources, or information technology.
Customer retention	Customer retention refers to the percentage of customers who return to a service provider or continue to purchase a manufactured product.
Productivity	Productivity refers to the total output of goods and services in a given period of time divided by work hours.
Communication	Communication refers to the social process in which two or more parties exchange information and share meaning.
Organizational design	The structuring of workers so that they can best accomplish the firm's goals is referred to as organizational design.
Organizational learning	Organizational learning is an area of knowledge within organizational theory that studies models and theories about the way an organization learns and adapts.
Organizational Behavior	The study of human behavior in organizational settings, the interface between human behavior and the organization, and the organization itself is called organizational behavior.
Continuous improvement	Constantly improving the way the organization does things so that customer needs can be better satisfied is referred to as continuous improvement.
Situational leadership model	Situational leadership model refers to a model of leadership proposed by Hersey and Blanchard that clarifies the interrelation between employee preparedness and effectiveness in leadership.
Situational leadership	Situational leadership refers to a leadership model, which argues that effective leadership involves matching the right combination of task-oriented and relationship-oriented behavior to the maturity level of subordinates.
Context	The effect of the background under which a message often takes on more and richer meaning is a context. Context is especially important in cross-cultural interactions because some cultures are said to be high context or low context.
Quality management	Quality management is a method for ensuring that all the activities necessary to design, develop and implement a product or service are effective and efficient with respect to the system and its performance.
Laissez-faire	Laissez-faire refers to the concept that the owners of business and industry should be allowed to compete without government intervention or regulation.
Accounting	The recording, classifying, summarizing, and interpreting of financial events and transactions to provide management and other interested parties the information they need to make good decisions is called accounting.
Marketing	The American Marketing Association suggests that Marketing is "the process of planning and executing the pricing, promotion, and distribution of goods, ideas, and services to create exchanges that satisfy individual and organizational goals."
Information system	An information system is a system whether automated or manual, that comprises people, machines, and/or methods organized to collect, process, transmit, and disseminate data that represent user information.

Forming	The first stage of team development, where the team is formed and the objectives for the team are set is referred to as forming.
Norming	The third stage of team development, where the team becomes a cohesive unit, and interdependence, trust, and cooperation are built is called norming.
Interdependence	The extent to which departments depend on each other for resources or materials to accomplish their tasks is referred to as interdependence.
Facilitator	A facilitator is someone who skilfully helps a group of people understand their common objectives and plan to achieve them without personally taking any side of the argument.
Continuous process	An uninterrupted production process in which long production runs turn out finished goods over time is called continuous process.
Cross-functional team	That which brings together persons from different functions to work on a common task is called a cross-functional team.
Preventive maintenance	Maintaining scheduled upkeep and improvement to equipment so equipment can actually improve with age is called the preventive maintenance.
Process improvement teams	Teams that are involved in identifying opportunities for improving select processes in a firm are process improvement teams.
Process improvement	Process improvement is the activity of elevating the performance of a process, especially that of a business process with regard to its goal.
Customer service	The ability of logistics management to satisfy users in terms of time, dependability, communication, and convenience is called the customer service.
Plan-do-check-act cycle	Plan-do-check-act cycle refers to a process for improvement pioneered by W. E. Deming. A cycle of activities designed to drive continuous improvement.
Problem-solving team	Typically 5 to 12 hourly employees from the same department who meet to discuss ways of improving quality, efficiency, and the work environment is referred to as problem-solving team.
Reengineering	The fundamental rethinking and radical redesign of organizational processes to achieve dramatic improvements in critical measures of performance is reengineering.
Product	Any physical good, service, or idea that satisfies a want or need is called product. Product in project management is a physical entity created as a result of project work.
Natural work groups	A term used to describe teams that are organized according to a common product, customer, or service are natural work groups.
Self-directed work team	Self-directed work team refers to a team made up of a group of employees who share responsibility for a complete product or process, or accomplishment of a significant part of a process. The self-directed work team literally directs its own work and manages its own work performance.
Task performance	The quantity and quality of work produced is referred to as the task performance. Actions taken to ensure that the work group reaches its goals.
Computer-aided design	Computer-aided design is the use of a wide range of computer-based tools that assist engineers, architects and other design professionals in their design activities. It is the main geometry authoring tool within the Product Lifecycle Management process and involves both software and sometimes special-purpose hardware.
Computer-integrated	Computer-integrated manufacturing is totally automated production in which all manufacturing processes are integrated and controlled by a central computer and is the union of computer-

manufacturing	aided design with computer-aided manufacturing.
Manufacturing	Manufacturing is the transformation of raw materials into finished goods for sale, by means of tools and a processing medium, and including all intermediate processes involving the production or finishing of component parts.
Efficiency	Efficiency refers to the use of minimal resources, such as raw materials, money, and people-to produce a desired volume of output.
Virtual team	A group of physically dispersed people who work as a team via alternative communication modes is called virtual team.
Consortia	B2B marketplaces sponsored by a group of otherwise competitive enterprises in a specific industry like automobile manufacturing or airline operations are called a consortia.
Facilitation	Facilitation refers to helping a team or individual achieve a goal. Often used in meetings or with teams to help the teams achieve their objectives.
Team building	A term that describes the process of identifying roles for team members and helping the team members succeed in their roles is called team building.
Content	Content refers to all digital information included on a website, including the presentation form-text, video, audio, and graphics.
Action plan	Action plan refers to a written document that includes the steps the trainee and manager will take to ensure that training transfers to the job.
Human relations skills	Human relations skills refers to skills that involve communication and motivation; they enable managers to work through and with people.
Contribution	In business organization law, the cash or property contributed to a business by its owners is referred to as contribution.
Conflict resolution	Conflict resolution is the process of resolving a dispute or a conflict. Successful conflict resolution occurs by providing each side's needs, and adequately addressing their interests so that they are each satisfied with the outcome. Conflict resolution aims to end conflicts before they start or lead to physical fighting.
Micromanagement	Micromanagement refers to a pejorative term for supervising too closely. Any manager may be guilty of micromaaagement for refusing to allow subordinates to have any real authority or responsibility, thereby ensuring that subordinates can neither function as, or grow into, effective managers.
Active listening	Active listening is a way of "listening for meaning" in which the listener checks with the speaker to see that a statement has been correctly heard and understood. The goal of active listening is to improve mutual understanding.
Coordination	Coordination refers to the set of mechanisms used in an organization to link the actions of its subunits into a consistent pattern.
Competition	In business, competition occurs when rival organizations with similar products and services attempt to gain customers.
Effective communication	When the intended meaning equals the perceived meaning it is called effective communication.
Charter	Charter refers to an instrument or authority from the sovereign power bestowing the right or power to do business under the corporate form of organization. Also, the organic law of a city or town, and representing a portion of the statute law of the state.
Project charter	Project charter refers to a document showing the purposes, participants, goals, and authorizations for a project.

Current cost accounting	Current cost accounting refers to one of two methods of inflation-adjusted accounting approved by the Financial Accounting Standards Board in 1979. Financial statements are adjusted to the present, using current cost data, rather than an index. This is optional information may be shown in the firm's annual report.
Cost accounting	Cost accounting is the process of tracking, recording and analyzing costs associated with the products or activities of an organization, where cost is defined as required time or resources.
Intervention	A proceeding by which one not originally made a party to an action or suit is permitted, on his own application, to appear therein and join one of the original parties in maintaining his cause of action or defense, or to assert some cause of action against some or all of the parties to the proceeding as originally instituted is an intervention.
Critical path	The sequence of tasks that limit how quickly a project can be completed is referred to as critical path.
Program Evaluation and Review Technique	Program evaluation and review technique refers to a method for analyzing the tasks involved in completing a given project, estimating the time needed to complete each task, and identifying the minimum time needed to complete the total project.
Evaluation	The consumer's appraisal of the product or brand on important attributes is called evaluation.
Tiger teams	Teams with a specific defined goal and a short time frame to attain the goal are tiger teams.
New seven tools	Managerial tools that are used in total quality management are called the new seven tools.

Go to **Cram101.com** for the Practice Tests for this Chapter.
And, **NEVER** highlight a book again!

Inflation	A general rise in the prices of goods and services over time is an inflation. It is a change in some important measure of money which says either real or apparent value is falling.
Economy	The income, expenditures, and resources that affect the cost of running a business and household are called an economy.
Control charts	Control charts refer to tools for monitoring process variation.
Control chart	The control chart, also known as the 'Shewhart chart' or 'process-behavior chart' is a statistical tool intended to assess the nature of variation in a process and to facilitate forecasting and management. The control chart is one of the seven basic tools of quality control, which include the histogram, Pareto chart, check sheet, control chart, cause-and-effect diagram, flowchart, and scatter diagram.
Production	The creation of finished goods and services using the factors of production: land, labor, capital, entrepreneurship, and knowledge.
Statistical thinking	Deming's concept relating to databased decision-making is statistical thinking. Statistical thinking is the tendency to want to understand complete situational understanding over a wide range of data where several control factors may be interacting at once to produce and outcome.
Quality control	The measurement of products and services against set standards is referred to as quality control.
Consumer's risk	The risk of receiving a shipment of poor quality product and believing that it is good quality is referred to as consumer's risk.
Context	The effect of the background under which a message often takes on more and richer meaning is a context. Context is especially important in cross-cultural interactions because some cultures are said to be high context or low context.
Product	Any physical good, service, or idea that satisfies a want or need is called product. Product in project management is a physical entity created as a result of project work.
Management	Management characterizes the process of leading and directing all or part of an organization, often a business, through the deployment and manipulation of resources. Early twentieth-century management writer Mary Parker Follett defined management as "the art of getting things done through people."
Organizational control	Organizational control refers to the systematic process through which managers regulate organizational activities to make them consistent with expectations established in plans, targets, and standards of performance.
Centralization	A structural policy in which decision-making authority is concentrated at the top of the organizational hierarchy is referred to as centralization.
Authority	Authority in agency law, refers to an agent's ability to affect his principal's legal relations with third parties. Also used to refer to an actor's legal power or ability to do something. In addition, sometimes used to refer to a statute, case, or other legal source that justifies a particular result.
Empowerment	Giving employees the authority and responsibility to respond quickly to customer requests is called empowerment.
Exhibit	Exhibit refers to a copy of a written instrument on which a pleading is founded, annexed to the pleading and by reference made a part of it. Any paper or thing offered in evidence and marked for identification.
Assignable	Capable of being lawfully assigned or transferred to another is the assignable.

Acceptance sampling	Acceptance sampling refers to an inspection of a sample from a lot to decide whether to accept or not accept that lot.
Acceptance	The actual or implied receipt and retention of that which is tendered or offered is the acceptance.
In-process inspection	The practice of inspecting work, by the workers themselves, at each stage of the production process is an in-process inspection.
Sampling plan	In market research, the determination of how the data is to be collected, the interval of data collection, and the subjects from whom the data will be collected is called a sampling plan.
Statistical process control	Statistical process control is a method for achieving quality control in manufacturing processes. It is a set of methods using statistical tools such as mean, variance and others, to detect whether the process observed is under control.
X chart	A chart used to monitor the mean of a process for population values is called x chart.
Distribution	Distribution is one of the four aspects of marketing. A distribution business is the middleman between the manufacturer and retailer or (usually)in commercial or industrial the business customer.
Standard deviation	A measure of the spread or dispersion of a series of numbers around the expected value is the standard deviation. The standard deviation tells us how well the expected value represents a series of values.
Interest	Interest refers to the payment the issuer of the bond makes to the bondholders for use of the borrowed money. It is the return to capital achieved over time or as the result of an event.
Alignment	Term that refers to optimal coordination among disparate departments and divisions within a firm is referred to as alignment.
Just-in-time	Just In Time (JIT) is an inventory strategy implemented to improve the return on investment of a business by reducing in-process inventory and its associated costs.
Brainstorming	Brainstorming refers to a technique designed to overcome our natural tendency to evaluate and criticize ideas and thereby reduce the creative output of those ideas. People are encouraged to produce ideas/options without criticizing, often at a very fast pace to minimize our natural tendency to criticize.
Delegation	Delegation is the handing of a task over to another person, usually a subordinate. It is the assignment of authority and responsibility to another person to carry out specific activities.
Line-stop authority	The approval authority to stop a production line whenever a problem is detected is called line-stop authority.
Histogram	A representation of data in a bar chart format is called histogram.
S chart	Standard deviation chart for monitoring changes in process variation is referred to as an S chart.
Action steps	The part of a written affirmative plan that specifies what an employer plans to do to reduce underutilization of protected groups is referred to as action steps.
Continuous improvement	Constantly improving the way the organization does things so that customer needs can be better satisfied is referred to as continuous improvement.
Personnel	A collective term for all of the employees of an organization. Personnel is also commonly used to refer to the personnel management function or the organizational unit responsible for administering personnel programs.

Corporation	A form of business organization that is owned by owners, called shareholders, who have no inherent right to manage the business, and is managed by a board of directors that is elected by the shareholders is called a corporation.
Six Sigma	A means to 'delight the customer' by achieving quality through a highly disciplined process to focus on developing and delivering near-perfect products and services is called six sigma. Originally, it was defined as a metric for measuring defects and improving quality; and a methodology to reduce defect levels below 3.4 Defects Per (one) Million Opportunities (DPMO).
Taguchi	Taguchi is an engineer and statistician who developed a methodology for applying statistics to improve the quality of manufactured goods. Taguchi methods have been controversial among many conventional Western statisticians.
Stock	In financial terminology, stock is the capital raized by a corporation, through the issuance and sale of shares. A shareholder is any person or organization which owns one or more shares of a corporation's stock. The aggregate value of a corporation's issued shares is its market capitalization.
Manager	A person who is formally responsible for supporting the work efforts of other people is a manager.
Trial	An examination before a competent tribunal, according to the law of the land, of the facts or law put in issue in a cause, for the purpose of determining such issue is a trial. When the court hears and determines any issue of fact or law for the purpose of determining the rights of the parties, it may be considered a trial.
Off-line experimentation	Off-line experimentation refers to a method for determining the best configurations of processes. Usually uses a design of experiments format such as the Taguchi method or Plackett-Burman experiments.
Conformance	A dimension of quality that refers to the extent to which a product lies within an allowable range of deviation from its specification is called the conformance.

Go to **Cram101.com** for the Practice Tests for this Chapter.

Quality management	Quality management is a method for ensuring that all the activities necessary to design, develop and implement a product or service are effective and efficient with respect to the system and its performance.
Management	Management characterizes the process of leading and directing all or part of an organization, often a business, through the deployment and manipulation of resources. Early twentieth-century management writer Mary Parker Follett defined management as "the art of getting things done through people."
Structural attributes	Attributes having to do with physical characteristics of a product such as power steering or red paint are called structural attributes.
Product	Any physical good, service, or idea that satisfies a want or need is called product. Product in project management is a physical entity created as a result of project work.
Customer experience	The sum total of interactions that a customer has with a company's website is referred to as the customer experience.
Ethical attributes	Ethical attributes refer to attributes having to do with the honesty and goodness of people in a firm.
Accounting	The recording, classifying, summarizing, and interpreting of financial events and transactions to provide management and other interested parties the information they need to make good decisions is called accounting.
Production	The creation of finished goods and services using the factors of production: land, labor, capital, entrepreneurship, and knowledge.
Quality control	The measurement of products and services against set standards is referred to as quality control.
Control charts	Control charts refer to tools for monitoring process variation.
Control chart	The control chart, also known as the 'Shewhart chart' or 'process-behavior chart' is a statistical tool intended to assess the nature of variation in a process and to facilitate forecasting and management. The control chart is one of the seven basic tools of quality control, which include the histogram, Pareto chart, check sheet, control chart, cause-and-effect diagram, flowchart, and scatter diagram.
Interest	Interest refers to the payment the issuer of the bond makes to the bondholders for use of the borrowed money. It is the return to capital achieved over time or as the result of an event.
P chart	A chart used to monitor proportion defective is referred to as a p chart. It is an attribute control chart showing the fraction or percent of nonconforming data out of a given population.
NP chart	A chart used to monitor the number of items defective for a fixed sample size is referred to as a NP chart.
C chart	A chart used to monitor the number of defects in a production process is called c chart. A form of quality control chart by attributes in which the number of defects in the sample is plotted.
Distribution	Distribution is one of the four aspects of marketing. A distribution business is the middleman between the manufacturer and retailer or (usually)in commercial or industrial the business customer.
U chart	A chart used to monitor the number of defects in sequential production lots is called u chart.
Defects per unit	Total number of defects identified on all units divided by the number of units occurring in a

Go to **Cram101.com** for the Practice Tests for this Chapter.

117

particular product is called defects per unit.

Bathtub-shaped hazard function	Reliability model that shows that products are more likely to fail either very early in their useful life or very late in their useful life is a bathtub-shaped hazard function.
Warranty	A warranty is a promise that something sold is as factually stated or legally implied by the seller. A warranty may be express or implied. A breach of warranty occurs when the promise is broken, i.e., a product is defective or not as should be expected by a reasonable buyer.
Purchasing	Purchasing refers to the function in a firm that searches for quality material resources, finds the best suppliers, and negotiates the best price for goods and services.
Contract	A contract is a "promise" or an "agreement" that is enforced or recognized by the law. In the civil law, contracts are considered to be part of the general law of obligations. This article describes the law relating to contracts in common law jurisdictions.
Vendor	A person who sells property to a vendee is a vendor. The words vendor and vendee are more commonly applied to the seller and purchaser of real estate, and the words seller and buyer are more commonly applied to the seller and purchaser of personal property.
Component reliability	The propensity for a part to fail over a given time is referred to as component reliability.
Impossibility	A doctrine under which a party to a contract is relieved of his or her duty to perform when that performance has become impossible because of the occurrence of an event unforeseen at the time of contracting is referred to as impossibility.
Mistake	In contract law a mistake is incorrect understanding by one or more parties to a contract and may be used as grounds to invalidate the agreement. Common law has identified three different types of mistake in contract: unilateral mistake, mutual mistake, and common mistake.
Mean time to repair	The average time it takes for a product to be repaired is called mean time to repair.

Go to **Cram101.com** for the Practice Tests for this Chapter.

Six Sigma	A means to 'delight the customer' by achieving quality through a highly disciplined process to focus on developing and delivering near-perfect products and services is called six sigma. Originally, it was defined as a metric for measuring defects and improving quality; and a methodology to reduce defect levels below 3.4 Defects Per (one) Million Opportunities (DPMO).
Continuous improvement	Constantly improving the way the organization does things so that customer needs can be better satisfied is referred to as continuous improvement.
Contingency perspective	Contingency perspective suggests that, in most organizations, situations and outcomes are contingent on, or influenced by, other variables.
Standard deviation	A measure of the spread or dispersion of a series of numbers around the expected value is the standard deviation. The standard deviation tells us how well the expected value represents a series of values.
Product	Any physical good, service, or idea that satisfies a want or need is called product. Product in project management is a physical entity created as a result of project work.
Organizational learning	Organizational learning is an area of knowledge within organizational theory that studies models and theories about the way an organization learns and adapts.
Customer retention	Customer retention refers to the percentage of customers who return to a service provider or continue to purchase a manufactured product.
Inventory	Inventory refers to physical material purchased from suppliers, which may or may not be reworked for sale to customers. A unique element of services-the need for and cost of having a service provider available.
Yield	The interest rate that equates a future value or an annuity to a given present value is a yield.
Production	The creation of finished goods and services using the factors of production: land, labor, capital, entrepreneurship, and knowledge.
Management	Management characterizes the process of leading and directing all or part of an organization, often a business, through the deployment and manipulation of resources. Early twentieth-century management writer Mary Parker Follett defined management as "the art of getting things done through people."
Human resources	Human resources refers to the individuals within the firm, and to the portion of the firm's organization that deals with hiring, firing, training, and other personnel issues.
Participation	Participation refers to the process of giving employees a voice in making decisions about their own work.
Voice of the customer	A term that refers to the wants, opinions, perceptions, and desires of the customer is a voice of the customer.
Pareto analysis	Pareto analysis is a statistical technique in decision making used for selection of a limited number of tasks that produce significant overall effect.
Return on investment	Return on investment refers to the return a businessperson gets on the money he and other owners invest in the firm; for example, a business that earned $100 on a $1,000 investment would have a ROI of 10 percent: 100 divided by 1000.
Mentor	An experienced employee who supervises, coaches, and guides lower-level employees by introducing them to the right people and generally being their organizational sponsor is a mentor.
Business case	The business case addresses, at a high level, the business need that a project seeks to resolve. It includes the reasons for the project, the expected business benefits, the options

Go to **Cram101.com** for the Practice Tests for this Chapter.

considered (with reasons for rejecting or carrying forward each option), the expected costs of the project, a gap analysis and the expected risks.

Evaluation	The consumer's appraisal of the product or brand on important attributes is called evaluation.
Project risk assessment	Project risk assessment refers to a method for determining the propensity for a Six-Sigma project to achieve desired results.
Assessment	Collecting information and providing feedback to employees about their behavior, communication style, or skills is an assessment.
External failure costs	External failure costs refer to monetary losses associated with product failures after the customer has possession of the product. These may include warranty or field repair costs.
Failure costs	Two sets of costs-internal failure costs and external failure costs are called failure costs. Internal failure costs include those costs that are associated with failure during production, whereas external failure costs are associated with product failure after the production process.
Measure phase	Six-Sigma phase for collecting data is called the measure phase.
Defects per unit	Total number of defects identified on all units divided by the number of units occurring in a particular product is called defects per unit.
Defects per million opportunities	Defects per million opportunites constitutes a standard of measure that correlates failures of expected norms in any process. One failure per every million normative outcomes constitutes 1 defects per million opportunities.
Variance	In budgeting a variance is a difference between budgeted, planned or standard amount and the actual amount incurred/sold.
Improve phase	Improve phase refers to six-Sigma phase where improvements to products and processes are implemented. The Improve phase is when active experimentation is done to find (or verify) the root cause of a problem.
Brainstorming	Brainstorming refers to a technique designed to overcome our natural tendency to evaluate and criticize ideas and thereby reduce the creative output of those ideas. People are encouraged to produce ideas/options without criticizing, often at a very fast pace to minimize our natural tendency to criticize.
Off-line experimentation	Off-line experimentation refers to a method for determining the best configurations of processes. Usually uses a design of experiments format such as the Taguchi method or Plackett-Burman experiments.
Taguchi	Taguchi is an engineer and statistician who developed a methodology for applying statistics to improve the quality of manufactured goods. Taguchi methods have been controversial among many conventional Western statisticians.
Control phase	Six-Sigma phase where improved process performance is monitored is referred to as the control phase.
Trial	An examination before a competent tribunal, according to the law of the land, of the facts or law put in issue in a cause, for the purpose of determining such issue is a trial. When the court hears and determines any issue of fact or law for the purpose of determining the rights of the parties, it may be considered a trial.
Design of experiments	A practical application of a statistical tool that enables low cost experimental methods to optimise the performance of products and processes during development is the design of experiments.

Concept design	The process of determining which technologies and processes will be used to produce a product is called concept design.
Parameter design	Designing control factors such as product specifications and measurements for optimal product function is called parameter design.
Layout	Layout refers to the physical arrangement of the various parts of an advertisement including the headline, subheads, illustrations, body copy, and any identifying marks.
Customer service	The ability of logistics management to satisfy users in terms of time, dependability, communication, and convenience is called the customer service.
Acceptance	The actual or implied receipt and retention of that which is tendered or offered is the acceptance.
Statistical process control	Statistical process control is a method for achieving quality control in manufacturing processes. It is a set of methods using statistical tools such as mean, variance and others, to detect whether the process observed is under control.
Quality control	The measurement of products and services against set standards is referred to as quality control.
Quality loss function	A function that determines economic penalties that the customer incurs as a result of purchasing a nonconforming product is referred to as quality loss function.
Conformance	A dimension of quality that refers to the extent to which a product lies within an allowable range of deviation from its specification is called the conformance.
Ideal quality	A reference point identified by Taguchi for determining the quality level of a product or service is ideal quality.
Tangible	Having a physical existence is referred to as the tangible. Personal property other than real estate, such as cars, boats, stocks, or other assets.
Loss to society	Loss to society refers to, according to Taguchi, every time a dimension in a product varies from its target dimension.
Purchasing	Purchasing refers to the function in a firm that searches for quality material resources, finds the best suppliers, and negotiates the best price for goods and services.
Teamwork	That which occurs when group members work together in ways that utilize their skills well to accomplish a purpose is called teamwork.
Manager	A person who is formally responsible for supporting the work efforts of other people is a manager.
Facilitator	A facilitator is someone who skilfully helps a group of people understand their common objectives and plan to achieve them without personally taking any side of the argument.
Consideration	Consideration in contract law, a basic requirement for an enforceable agreement under traditional contract principles, defined in this text as legal value, bargained for and given in exchange for an act or promise. In corporation law, cash or property contributed to a corporation in exchange for shares, or a promise to contribute such cash or property.
Continuity	A media scheduling strategy where a continuous pattern of advertising is used over the time span of the advertising campaign is continuity.

Quality management	Quality management is a method for ensuring that all the activities necessary to design, develop and implement a product or service are effective and efficient with respect to the system and its performance.
Management	Management characterizes the process of leading and directing all or part of an organization, often a business, through the deployment and manipulation of resources. Early twentieth-century management writer Mary Parker Follett defined management as "the art of getting things done through people."
Organizational learning	Organizational learning is an area of knowledge within organizational theory that studies models and theories about the way an organization learns and adapts.
Quality control	The measurement of products and services against set standards is referred to as quality control.
Productivity	Productivity refers to the total output of goods and services in a given period of time divided by work hours.
Product	Any physical good, service, or idea that satisfies a want or need is called product. Product in project management is a physical entity created as a result of project work.
Stock	In financial terminology, stock is the capital raized by a corporation, through the issuance and sale of shares. A shareholder is any person or organization which owns one or more shares of a corporation's stock. The aggregate value of a corporation's issued shares is its market capitalization.
Complexity	The technical sophistication of the product and hence the amount of understanding required to use it is referred to as complexity. It is the opposite of simplicity.
Teamwork	That which occurs when group members work together in ways that utilize their skills well to accomplish a purpose is called teamwork.
Context	The effect of the background under which a message often takes on more and richer meaning is a context. Context is especially important in cross-cultural interactions because some cultures are said to be high context or low context.
Forming	The first stage of team development, where the team is formed and the objectives for the team are set is referred to as forming.
Brainstorming	Brainstorming refers to a technique designed to overcome our natural tendency to evaluate and criticize ideas and thereby reduce the creative output of those ideas. People are encouraged to produce ideas/options without criticizing, often at a very fast pace to minimize our natural tendency to criticize.
Business case	The business case addresses, at a high level, the business need that a project seeks to resolve. It includes the reasons for the project, the expected business benefits, the options considered (with reasons for rejecting or carrying forward each option), the expected costs of the project, a gap analysis and the expected risks.
Options	Options give the owner the right but not the obligation to buy or sell an underlying security at a set price for a given time period.
Training needs assessment	A process for gathering organizational data relative to finding areas where training is most needed is referred to as training needs assessment.
Needs assessment	The process used to determine if training is necessary is called needs assessment.
Assessment	Collecting information and providing feedback to employees about their behavior, communication style, or skills is an assessment.
Strategic	The process of determining the major goals of the organization and the policies and

planning	strategies for obtaining and using resources to achieve those goals is called strategic planning.
Human resources	Human resources refers to the individuals within the firm, and to the portion of the firm's organization that deals with hiring, firing, training, and other personnel issues.
Strategic plan	The formal document that presents the ways and means by which a strategic goal will be achieved is a strategic plan. A long-term flexible plan that does not regulate activities but rather outlines the means to achieve certain results, and provides the means to alter the course of action should the desired ends change.
Alignment	Term that refers to optimal coordination among disparate departments and divisions within a firm is referred to as alignment.
Inventory	Inventory refers to physical material purchased from suppliers, which may or may not be reworked for sale to customers. A unique element of services-the need for and cost of having a service provider available.
Acceptance	The actual or implied receipt and retention of that which is tendered or offered is the acceptance.
Strategic alliance	Strategic alliance refers to a long-term partnership between two or more companies established to help each company build competitive market advantages.
Performance appraisal	An evaluation in which the performance level of employees is measured against established standards to make decisions about promotions, compenzation, additional training, or firing is referred to as performance appraisal.
Contingency approach	Contingency approach refers to the dominant perspective in organizational behavior, it argues that there's no single best way to manage behavior. What 'works' in any given context depends on the complex interplay between a variety of person and situational factors.
Bottom line	Bottom line refers to the last line in a profit and loss statement; it refers to net profit.
Evaluation	The consumer's appraisal of the product or brand on important attributes is called evaluation.
Task needs assessment	The process of assessing the skills that are needed within a firm is called task needs assessment.
Training and development	All attempts to improve productivity by increasing an employee's ability to perform is training and development.
Manager	A person who is formally responsible for supporting the work efforts of other people is a manager.
Facilitation	Facilitation refers to helping a team or individual achieve a goal. Often used in meetings or with teams to help the teams achieve their objectives.
Flowchart	A pictorial representation of the progression of a particular process over time is called a flowchart. They are commonly used in business/economic presentations to help the audience visualize the content better, or to find flaws in the process
Workflow	Workflow refers to automated systems that electronically route documents to the next person in the process.
Self-direction	A term that refers to providing autonomy to employees in terms of facilitating their own training needs is called self-direction.
Design phase	The phase in the instructional system design process where learning objectives, tests, and the required skills and knowledge for a task are constructed and sequenced is the design phase.

Interest	Interest refers to the payment the issuer of the bond makes to the bondholders for use of the borrowed money. It is the return to capital achieved over time or as the result of an event.
Holding	The holding is a court's determination of a matter of law based on the issue presented in the particular case. In other words: under this law, with these facts, this result.
Controlling	A management function that involves determining whether or not an organization is progressing toward its goals and objectives, and taking corrective action if it is not is called controlling.
Computer-based training	Computer-based training refers to a form of training that uses specialized software, known as courseware, to address specific topics.
Just-in-time	Just In Time (JIT) is an inventory strategy implemented to improve the return on investment of a business by reducing in-process inventory and its associated costs.
Tangibles	Dimension of service quality-appearance of physical facilities, equipment, personnel, and communication materials are called tangibles.
Tangible	Having a physical existence is referred to as the tangible. Personal property other than real estate, such as cars, boats, stocks, or other assets.
Production	The creation of finished goods and services using the factors of production: land, labor, capital, entrepreneurship, and knowledge.
Customer service	The ability of logistics management to satisfy users in terms of time, dependability, communication, and convenience is called the customer service.
Profound organizational learning	Quality-based learning that occurs as people discover the causes of errors, defects, and poor customer service in a firm is profound organizational learning.
Appraisal costs	Expenses associated with the direct costs of measuring quality are called appraisal costs.
Internal failure costs	Internal failure costs refers to losses that occur while the product is in possession of the producer. These include rework and scrap costs.
Internal failure cost	An internal failure cost refers to any loss that occurs while a product is in possession of the producer. These include rework and scrap costs.
Failure costs	Two sets of costs-internal failure costs and external failure costs are called failure costs. Internal failure costs include those costs that are associated with failure during production, whereas external failure costs are associated with product failure after the production process.
Compensation	A payment that is given or recieved as reparation for a service or loss is referred to as compensation.
Knowledge-growth systems	A compenzation system that increases an employee's pay as he or she establishes competencies at different levels relating to job knowledge in a single job classification is referred to as knowledge-growth systems.
Skill-based pay	Pay based on the skills employees acquire and are capable of using is skill-based pay.
Administration	Administration refers to the management and direction of the affairs of governments and institutions; a collective term for all policymaking officials of a government; the execution and implementation of public policy.
Economy	The income, expenditures, and resources that affect the cost of running a business and household are called an economy.
Insurance	A means for persons and businesses to protect themselves against the risk of loss is

insurance.

Quality management	Quality management is a method for ensuring that all the activities necessary to design, develop and implement a product or service are effective and efficient with respect to the system and its performance.
Management	Management characterizes the process of leading and directing all or part of an organization, often a business, through the deployment and manipulation of resources. Early twentieth-century management writer Mary Parker Follett defined management as "the art of getting things done through people."
Competitor	Other organizations in the same industry or type of business that provide a good or service to the same set of customers is referred to as a competitor.
Complexity	The technical sophistication of the product and hence the amount of understanding required to use it is referred to as complexity. It is the opposite of simplicity.
Empathy	Empathy refers to dimension of service quality-caring individualized attention provided to customers.
Customer service	The ability of logistics management to satisfy users in terms of time, dependability, communication, and convenience is called the customer service.
Production	The creation of finished goods and services using the factors of production: land, labor, capital, entrepreneurship, and knowledge.
Manager	A person who is formally responsible for supporting the work efforts of other people is a manager.
Empowerment	Giving employees the authority and responsibility to respond quickly to customer requests is called empowerment.
Authority	Authority in agency law, refers to an agent's ability to affect his principal's legal relations with third parties. Also used to refer to an actor's legal power or ability to do something. In addition, sometimes used to refer to a statute, case, or other legal source that justifies a particular result.
Restructuring	Restructuring is the corporate management term for the act of partially dismantling and reorganizing a company for the purpose of making it more efficient and therefore more profitable.
Reengineering	The fundamental rethinking and radical redesign of organizational processes to achieve dramatic improvements in critical measures of performance is reengineering.
Economy	The income, expenditures, and resources that affect the cost of running a business and household are called an economy.
Organizational learning	Organizational learning is an area of knowledge within organizational theory that studies models and theories about the way an organization learns and adapts.
Capital	Contributions of money and other property to a business made by the owners of the business are capital.
Needs assessment	The process used to determine if training is necessary is called needs assessment.
Assessment	Collecting information and providing feedback to employees about their behavior, communication style, or skills is an assessment.
Customer contact	Customer contact refers to a characteristic of services that notes that customers tend to be more involved in the production of services than they are in manufactured goods.
Trust	Trust refers to a legal relationship in which a person who has legal title to property has the duty to hold it for the use or benefit of another person. The term is also used in a general sense to mean confidence reposed in one person by another.

Control system	A control system is a device or set of devices that manage the behavior of other devices. Some devices or systems are not controllable.A control system is an interconnection of components connected or related in such a manner as to command, direct, or regulate itself or another system.
Accounting	The recording, classifying, summarizing, and interpreting of financial events and transactions to provide management and other interested parties the information they need to make good decisions is called accounting.
Customer retention	Customer retention refers to the percentage of customers who return to a service provider or continue to purchase a manufactured product.
Marketing	The American Marketing Association suggests that Marketing is "the process of planning and executing the pricing, promotion, and distribution of goods, ideas, and services to create exchanges that satisfy individual and organizational goals."
Loyalty	Marketers tend to define customer loyalty as making repeat purchases. Some argue that it should be defined attitudinally as a strongly positive feeling about the brand.
Brand loyalty	The degree to which customers are satisfied, like the brand, and are committed to further purchase is referred to as brand loyalty.
Brand	A name, symbol, or design that identifies the goods or services of one seller or group of sellers and distinguishes them from the goods and services of competitors is a brand.
Product	Any physical good, service, or idea that satisfies a want or need is called product. Product in project management is a physical entity created as a result of project work.
E-commerce	The sale of goods and services by computer over the Internet is referred to as the e-commerce.
Information system	An information system is a system whether automated or manual, that comprises people, machines, and/or methods organized to collect, process, transmit, and disseminate data that represent user information.
Purchasing	Purchasing refers to the function in a firm that searches for quality material resources, finds the best suppliers, and negotiates the best price for goods and services.
Coordination	Coordination refers to the set of mechanisms used in an organization to link the actions of its subunits into a consistent pattern.
Quality assurance	Those activities associated with assuring the quality of a product or service is called quality assurance.
Quality control	The measurement of products and services against set standards is referred to as quality control.
Enterprise capabilities	Enterprise capabilities refer to capabilities that make firms unique and attractive to customers.
Corporation	A form of business organization that is owned by owners, called shareholders, who have no inherent right to manage the business, and is managed by a board of directors that is elected by the shareholders is called a corporation.
Competency	Competency refers to a person's ability to understand the nature of the transaction and the consequences of entering into it at the time the contract was entered into.
Productivity	Productivity refers to the total output of goods and services in a given period of time divided by work hours.
Systems view	A management viewpoint that focuses on the interactions between the various components that combine to produce a product or service is called systems view. The systems view focuses

Go to **Cram101.com** for the Practice Tests for this Chapter.

	management on the system as the cause of quality problems.
Alignment	Term that refers to optimal coordination among disparate departments and divisions within a firm is referred to as alignment.
Policy	Similar to a script in that a policy can be a less than completely rational decision-making method. Involves the use of a pre-existing set of decision steps for any problem that presents itself.
Continuous improvement	Constantly improving the way the organization does things so that customer needs can be better satisfied is referred to as continuous improvement.
Benchmarking	Discovering how others do something better than your own firm so you can imitate or leapfrog competition is called benchmarking.
Industry	Industry refers to a group of firms offering products that are close substitutes for each other.
Categorizing	The act of placing strengths and weaknesses into categories in generic internal assessment is called categorizing.
Audit	Audit refers to the verification of a company's books and records pursuant to federal securities laws, state laws, and stock exchange rules that must be performed by an independent CPA.
Competitive advantage	A business is said to have a competitive advantage when its unique strengths, often based on cost, quality, time, and innovation, offer consumers a greater percieved value and there by diffetiating it from its competitors.
Evaluation	The consumer's appraisal of the product or brand on important attributes is called evaluation.
Cost leadership	A type of competitive strategy with which the organization aggressively seeks efficient facilities, cuts costs, and employs tight cost controls to be more efficient than competitors is referred to as cost leadership.
Compliance	A type of influence process where a receiver accepts the position advocated by a source to obtain favorable outcomes or to avoid punishment is the compliance.
Acceptance	The actual or implied receipt and retention of that which is tendered or offered is the acceptance.
Generally accepted accounting principles	Standards for the preparation and presentation of financial statements are called generally accepted accounting principles.
Verification	Verification refers to the final stage of the creative process where the validity or truthfulness of the insight is determined. The feedback portion of communication in which the receiver sends a message to the source indicating receipt of the message and the degree to which he or she understood the message.
Assignment	A transfer of property or some right or interest is referred to as assignment.
Preparation	Preparation refers to usually the first stage in the creative process. It includes education and formal training.
Prejudice	Prejudice is, as the name implies, the process of "pre-judging" something. It implies coming to a judgment on a subject before learning where the preponderance of evidence actually lies, or forming a judgment without direct experience.
Consideration	Consideration in contract law, a basic requirement for an enforceable agreement under

Go to **Cram101.com** for the Practice Tests for this Chapter.

traditional contract principles, defined in this text as legal value, bargained for and given in exchange for an act or promise. In corporation law, cash or property contributed to a corporation in exchange for shares, or a promise to contribute such cash or property.

Operational auditing	Modern auditing practices that focus on operational efficiencies are referred to as operational auditing.
QS 9000	A supplier development program developed by a Daimler Chrysler/Ford/General Motors supplier requirement task force is the QS 9000. The purpose of the QS 9000 is to provide a common standard and a set of procedures for the suppliers of the three companies.
Applicant	In many tribunal and administrative law suits, the person who initiates the claim is called the applicant.
Strategic plan	The formal document that presents the ways and means by which a strategic goal will be achieved is a strategic plan. A long-term flexible plan that does not regulate activities but rather outlines the means to achieve certain results, and provides the means to alter the course of action should the desired ends change.
Conformance	A dimension of quality that refers to the extent to which a product lies within an allowable range of deviation from its specification is called the conformance.
Check sheet	A data-gathering tool that can be used in forming histograms is a check sheet. The check sheet can be either tabular or schematic.
External validation	External validation refers to using benchmarking as a way to ensure that a firm's current practices are comparable to those being used by benchmark firms.
Strategic planning	The process of determining the major goals of the organization and the policies and strategies for obtaining and using resources to achieve those goals is called strategic planning.
Estate	An estate is the totality of the legal rights, interests, entitlements and obligations attaching to property. In the context of wills and probate, it refers to the totality of the property which the deceased owned or in which some interest was held.
Deming prize	Japanese quality award for individuals and groups that have contributed to the field of quality control is called the deming prize.